JUKE BOX HERO

My Five Decades in Rock 'n' Roll

Lou Gramm

with Scott Pitoniak

TRIUMPH
BOOKS

This book has previously been catalogued with the Library of Congress as:

Gramm, Lou.

Juke box hero : my five decades in rock 'n' roll / Lou Gramm, with Scott Pitoniak.

pages cm

Includes index.

ISBN 978-1-60078-759-1

1. Gramm, Lou. 2. Rock musicians--United States--Biography. I. Pitoniak, Scott. II. Title.

ML420.G805A3 2013

782.42166092--dc23

[B]   2012042534

This book is available in quantity at special discounts for your group or organization. For further information, contact:

Triumph Books LLC

814 North Franklin Street

Chicago, Illinois 60610

(312) 337-0747

Fax (312) 280-5470

www.triumphbooks.com

Printed in U.S.A.

ISBN: 978-1-62937-758-2

Design by Sue Knopf

Photos courtesy of the author unless otherwise indicated

*To my wife, Robyn; my children,
Luciana, Natalie, Joe, Nicolas,
and Matthew; my parents, Ben
and Nikki Grammatico; my
brother, Ben Grammatico, and
his wife, Francesca; my late
father-in-law, Leonard Butera;
my brothers-in-law, Ron and
Bob Butera; all my fans around
the world; and my Lord and
Savior, Jesus Christ!*
                    —Lou Gramm

*To Beth, Amy, Christopher,
Camryn, Peyton and Sassy –
you guys rock my world!*
                    —Scott Pitoniak

Contents

Acknowledgments vii

Introduction ix

1 A Harmonious Beginning. 1

2 Banding Together. 13

3 The Black Sheep of Rock 31

4 A Long, Long Way From Home. 47

5 No Foreigner to Success. 69

6 Less is More 91

7 I Want to Know What Foreigner's Future Is 109

8 Taking Steps Down the Road to Redemption 133

9 Battling Back from Death's Doorstep. 151

10 An End and a Beginning 169

Epilogue 189

Appendix: Lou Gramm's Discography. 223

Sources 229

Index. 231

About the Authors 241

Acknowledgments

A book, like an album or a concert performance, requires a team effort. A lot of people, including many who perform anonymously behind the scenes, have to work in harmony to pull it off.

With that in mind, the authors would like the following to take a bow:

- Triumph Books, especially Noah Amstadter, Mitch Rogatz, Tom Bast, Adam Motin and Jesse Jordan for believing in this project and helping it come to fruition, both in hard cover and paperback;
- Robyn Grammatico and Bob Golino, for arranging numerous interviews, providing background materials and photographs, and keeping the process moving forward during Lou's often hectic schedule;
- Ben Grammatico and Dave Kane for sharing their insights, which spurred several additional anecdotes by Lou that really fleshed out the book.

Juke Box Hero

Standing in the rain, with his head hung low
Couldn't get a ticket; it was a sold-out show

Heard the roar of the crowd. He could picture the scene
Put his ear to the wall, then like a distant scream

He heard one guitar. Just blew him away
Saw stars in his eyes and the very next day

Bought a beat-up six string in a second-hand store
Didn't know how to play it, but he knew for sure

That one guitar felt good in his hands
Didn't take long. To understand

Just one guitar, slung way down low
Was a one-way ticket. Only one-way to go

So he started rockin'. Ain't never gonna stop
Gotta keep on rockin'. Someday he's gonna make it to the top
And be a Juke Box Hero. Got stars in his eyes
He's a Juke Box Hero
He took one guitar. Stars in his eyes
Juke Box Hero. He'll come alive tonight

In a town without a name, in a heavy downpour
Thought he passed his own shadow by the backstage door

Like a trip through the past to that day in the rain
And that one guitar made his whole life change

Now he needs to keep on rockin'; he just can't stop
Gotta keep on rockin'. That boy has got to stay on top

And be a Juke Box Hero. Got stars in his eyes
He's a Juke Box Hero. Got stars in his eyes
Yeah Juke Box Hero. Got stars in his eyes

With that one guitar, he'll come alive
Come alive tonight
So he started rockin'. Ain't never gonna stop
Gotta keep on rockin'—someday he's gonna make it to the top

And be a Juke Box Hero. Got stars in his eyes
He's a Juke Box Hero, Juke Box Hero, Juke Box Hero
Got stars in his eyes. Stars in his eyes

(Written by Lou Gramm and Mick Jones.)

Introduction

As 1996 drew to a close, I began waking up periodically with these splitting headaches that were far worse than any hangover I'd experienced during the years when booze and drugs ruled my life. There were mornings when it felt like someone had put my skull in a vise…mornings when I thought my head was going to explode into a million pieces. The pain was beyond excruciating.

A friend mentioned that maybe the headaches were being caused by carbon monoxide in our house, so I called the local utility company, but their tests showed nothing out of the ordinary.

In addition to the headaches, I started experiencing bouts of short- and long-term memory loss. I'd go to call my parents and halfway through dialing my mind would go blank. Here was a number I had called thousands of times—a number that hadn't changed in 20 years—and suddenly it was as if someone had erased the digits from my mind. I'd have to pull out my personal phone book and look up the number. Around this time, I also began forgetting the names of people I had known for decades.

I'd run into close friends and relatives, and I would struggle to come up with their names. At first, I would try to make light of it. I'd joke that I had too many lyrics dancing around in my head or that I was experiencing a senior moment, even though I was only 46 years old.

Compounding matters, I began suffering from blurred vision. Yeah, I know, that was kind of ironic. Here I am, the guy who wrote and sang the hit "Double Vision," suddenly having difficulties seeing clearly.

For several weeks, I deluded myself and others into thinking that all these health issues were merely temporary—a result of stress and fatigue—and that, with a little rest, they would disappear and I'd be my old self again. But my problems only worsened as I prepared to rejoin Foreigner after the band members had taken a short hiatus to recharge our batteries. My fiancée, who had grown increasingly frustrated with my forgetfulness, finally convinced me to stop being so pig-headed. So the day before we were scheduled to leave for Japan to begin our 1997 world summer tour (I actually had my bags packed), I went to my doctor, and he immediately scheduled an MRI. The X-rays of my brain detected an egg-sized tumor with tentacle-like appendages in the frontal lobe. The medical term for it was craniopharyngioma. The appendages were wrapped around my pituitary gland and optic nerve. The good news was that the tumor was benign. The bad news was that it was in my brain and growing.

I wound up meeting with the head of neurology at Strong Memorial Hospital in my hometown of Rochester, New York, and after an examination of the MRIs he told me that my situation was grave. He believed there was a remote chance they could operate on it, but my odds of surviving weren't good, and if I did survive I likely would suffer collateral damage during the surgery that would dramatically alter my cognition and memory.

He suggested I fly to New York to meet with a nationally renowned neurologist who was an expert in these types of tumors. I took his advice, and the specialist wound up giving me an even grimmer prognosis. He said the tumor was inoperable and that I should get my things in order. I walked out of his Manhattan office feeling numb from head to toe.

I had just been given a death sentence at the ripe old age of 46.

I was returning home to die.

MRI folder in hand, I hailed a cab and asked the driver to take me to the airport. Oblivious to the sights and sounds of the big city zipping by, my mind began to wander aimlessly. My life was literally flashing before my eyes.

I thought about that time when, as a 12-year-old, I was playing a big band beat on my drum set in the basement and my father, in a moment of inspiration and joy, grabbed his trumpet for the first time in years and began playing along with me. Next thing I knew, my mom, who had a voice like a bird, started singing at the top of her lungs as she descended the stairs, swinging a dish towel above her head.

I remembered how in 1978, just two years after going on public assistance and scrubbing floors in the Monroe County Office Building, I was on stage with the neophyte rock band Foreigner at the old War Memorial in my hometown, belting out the lyrics to "Feels Like the First Time," hearing 10,000 maniacs chanting "Lou! Lou! Lou!" and thinking dreams really do come true—even for a working-class kid from little old Rochester.

And I recalled the bad times, too. I remembered waking up in too many strange hotel rooms, groggy from a night of post-concert boozing, drugging, and carousing, feeling guilty about the time away from my wife and two young boys, haunted by my father's warning that music was a great pastime but a bad career choice for a husband and a dad.

As we approached JFK, I couldn't help but wonder if the self-destructive lifestyle I once led had finally caught up to me. Perhaps the years of drinking and drugs had caused this monster to surface and grow in my head, and payback time had arrived, even though I had cleaned up my act six years earlier.

In the days following my no-hope prognosis, I walked around feeling more like a zombie than a Juke Box Hero. I found it difficult to concentrate and stay focused on anything or anybody for very long. I spent plenty of time preoccupied with either the past or the future. It was like the present didn't exist.

One night, I was sitting in front of the television set. The popular ABC news show *20/20* was on, but I wasn't paying much attention until they began interviewing a brain surgeon from Boston who was having success removing tumors previously thought to be inoperable. My ears perked up, and I began listening intently as Dr. Peter Black explained how lasers could venture into super sensitive areas where scalpels could not, and they could do so without causing collateral damage. At the end of the show, they flashed Dr. Black's contact information on the screen. Grasping for any straw I could find, I called first thing the next morning. I was worried he was going to be so backed up that it would be months before he'd be able to see me, and I had been told that my tumor was expanding so rapidly that I didn't have months to live. His secretary listened to my story and told me there had been a cancelation (in other words, someone had died), and she wanted to know if I could be there the next day.

I firmly believe God had intervened.

I arrived in Boston on a Tuesday, underwent more MRIs, and met with Dr. Black, who told me in his soft, reassuring voice that I had a better-than-average chance of not only surviving the laser surgery but living a relatively normal life.

As they wheeled me to the operating room at Brigham & Women's Hospital that Thursday morning, I was deep in prayer. I told the Lord, "Let your will be done. If you mean to take me now, I'm ready. And if you want me to continue my life in this realm, I'm ready for that challenge, too."

My fate was in someone else's hands, and I was at peace with that.

1

A Harmonious Beginning

That I would choose a career in music is hardly a mystery because I come from a family of musicians. In fact, it was music that brought my mom and dad together in the first place. Ben Grammatico (yes, that's my real last name, and I'll tell you why it was changed later) was a second-generation Italian-American who went to Madison High School in Rochester. My mom, Nikki Masetta, had attended Franklin High School, Madison's hated cross-town rival. The story goes that Dad, an accomplished trumpet player, landed a gig with a swing band in the early 1940s and wound up meeting my mom while performing at a concert. They started dating, fell in love, and got married. And when my dad broke away to form his own band—the 16-piece Sonny James Orchestra—he asked Mom, a gifted singer, to become the lead vocalist.

Their love of music was instilled by their parents and was passed down to me and my two brothers. Some of my earliest and fondest memories are of spending Sundays—"Sauce Sundays," we called them—at my grandparents' houses. I can still smell the enticing aroma of homemade spaghetti sauce wafting through the air, and I can still hear the voices of Sinatra and Caruso booming from a big, old wooden Philco radio that was tuned to *The Italian Hour*.

My grandparents on both sides of the family arrived with thousands of other immigrants at Ellis Island in the early 1900s. One of my grandfathers—Louis Grammatico, whom I'm named after—was actually sponsored by a Protestant church. Apparently, churches would pay for an immigrant's boat fare and provide food and a place to live if he or she agreed to convert. So Grandpa Grammatico wound up becoming a Baptist, and that occasionally resulted in some heated religious discussions at those Sunday get-togethers because my mom and her family were raised Catholic.

My grandparents worked as migrant farm workers upon settling in this country. I remember Grandpa Grammatico telling us that he started his American journey by picking cabbage in the Southern Tier region of New York State before migrating north to Rochester. He talked about the Spartan conditions when he first arrived. Yes, the sponsor families provided shelter, but it was often a shack with a dirt floor and no plumbing. But he and the other immigrants were hardy souls and were thrilled just to be in a land where the opportunities seemed boundless. They survived and later thrived. I'm always amazed when I think back to what they had to overcome.

Although my dad's local band was successful, there was never a time when it became a full-time occupation for him and my mom. It was always a side venture, a hobby, an avocation—something he did to pick up extra cash on the weekends and blow off a little steam. And that was something he harped on with me and my brothers. "You can love music," he said, "but don't ever think about making a life out of it; it's too hard on families." I must have heard those words a thousand times. And they would haunt me later when the often lonely, empty life of a rock star got the better of me.

Mom dropped out of Dad's band when she started having kids. And Dad gave it up in the mid-1950s because the weekend gigs on top of his regular job were running him ragged and keeping him away from our family too much.

Dad's real job was building metal filing cabinets for the Rochester-based company Yarman & Erbe. It wasn't easy work. He put in a lot of backbreaking hours at the factory, and I can remember him coming home dog-tired with grease stains on his T-shirt and gauze wrapped around hands bloodied from the flying shards he encountered while cutting the sheet metal to build the cabinets. My older brother, Ben, and I got a chance to see what he went through firsthand when Dad brought us into work with him on those Saturdays when he picked up overtime. I was a little freaked out because it was so noisy and hot in there. They'd have the windows open, but it didn't help. Even in the winter time it was hotter than the blazes, just like a sauna. I could see why my dad was so exhausted.

Looking back, I'd say I had a pretty normal childhood—nothing terribly out of the ordinary. I was born in Rochester on May 2, 1950, the second of three boys, and I spent my first 11 years living in neighborhoods on the city's west side. When I was three years old, we moved to a section of the city known as the 19th Ward, which was mostly populated by Italian-American families. It was definitely a blue-collar neighborhood, and it was safe. My friends and I spent hours upon hours riding our bikes all over the place without a care in the world. (It was the 1950s and no one seemed too worried about kids being abducted back then.) We were always outdoors doing something, and some of my most cherished recollections are of playing baseball either in sandlot games with my buddies at the diamond at School 37 or in Little League games at Genesee Valley Park several blocks away. Baseball definitely was my first love, and my summer routine revolved around playing ball. I'd have my breakfast, grab my glove, say goodbye to my mom, and head to the schoolyard, returning home only for lunch and dinner. And when I wasn't at the diamond, you'd often see me firing a tennis ball at the house, pretending I was Don Newcombe or Sandy Koufax, the thudding of each pitch against the wall driving my poor mom nuts.

My dad was the one who got me interested in baseball. One of the first things he would do when he got home from work was plop himself down in his easy chair and read the paper. He'd always go to the sports section first and pore over the major league box scores. I was intrigued by his fascination with these funny-looking little boxes of type filled with names and numbers that were foreign to me. One day when I was about four or five, he sat me on his lap and taught me how to read a box score. He showed me how they measured the statistical performance of each player from the previous day's games, and it wasn't long before I became as mesmerized by the names and numbers as he was. Eventually, I would grab the paper before he got home, and when he entered the door I would give him an update on how the players from my favorite team, the Brooklyn Dodgers, had fared.

The Dodgers lineup in the 1950s was loaded with talented athletes such as Jackie Robinson, Gil Hodges, Roy Campanella, and PeeWee Reese. But my favorite player was their stylish centerfielder, Duke Snider. It seemed like every day I checked the box scores he'd have two or three hits and a double or a homer. I couldn't wait to get the paper to see how Duke had done. Sadly, most of my friends were Yankees fans, and I'd have to put up with their arrogance and obnoxiousness. They incessantly reminded me that their team was a perennial World Series champion, usually at the expense of my Dodgers, who were a great ballclub but always seemed to find a way to break our hearts in the end.

One of the worst moments of my childhood occurred when I was seven years old and learned that the Dodgers would be leaving Brooklyn and moving permanently to Los Angeles. I was as devastated as the folks who lived next door to Ebbets Field. I continued to root for the Duke of Flatbush, even though he was now 3,000 miles away, but my love for the Dodgers eventually faded. In 1962, when the National League returned to New York in the form of the Mets, I switched my allegiances to them. Like Brooklyn before them, the Mets sure knew how to test one's loyalty, but they also provided me with some great moments, too. The '69 Miracle Mets gave me one of my great thrills, stunning the sports world by upsetting the heavily favored Baltimore Orioles in the World Series. That amazing team was led by future Hall of Fame pitcher Tom Seaver. In one of those interesting life-coming-full-circle stories, I wound up meeting Tom Terrific at Citi Field during the summer of 2011. I was there to sing the National Anthem before a Mets game, and Seaver came up to me afterward and told me had been a huge fan of mine during my Foreigner days. And I told him that the feeling was mutual, that I was a huge fan of his and that he had given me some very entertaining and memorable moments along the way.

I also enjoyed other sports, as well, especially boxing and football. I later became a diehard Buffalo Bills fan—still am. My allegiance to the old, "Wait Until Next Year" Brooklyn Dodgers clearly had prepared me for the near misses the Bills would suffer during their Super Bowl years of the early 1990s. Being an Upstate New York guy, I also began following Syracuse University football and basketball closely and reveled in the Orangemen's national hoops championship season in 2003.

• • •

Our parents encouraged each of us boys to take up an instrument. My choice was drums because it looked like a lot of fun banging away with those sticks. I didn't even have a snare drum at first—we couldn't afford one—but my dad wound up making me a practice pad, which essentially was a rubberized playing surface over a piece of wood. Dad was a pretty ingenious guy. He used a piece of floor tile for the battering surface. It worked out well. I was about eight years old when I started beating on my practice pad and began taking drum lessons at Music Lovers in downtown Rochester. By age 11, I had become pretty proficient, and my percussion teacher urged me to try out for the All-County scholastic orchestra. To my surprise I earned a spot, which was a big thrill because the orchestra consisted mostly of kids in grades 9–12. In the ninth grade I also was encouraged to audition for admission to the prestigious Eastman School of Music, which was founded by George Eastman, the film magnate whose Rochester-based Eastman Kodak Company revolutionized the film and camera industry. I auditioned for John Beck, Rochester's renowned master percussionist. He was impressed and loved the way I played. He said I was a talented young drummer and he was going to do his best to see that I received a scholarship. A few weeks later we received a good news/bad news letter from Mr. Beck. The good news was that I had been accepted into the school; the bad news was that the school had already exceeded its scholarship limit and wouldn't be able to offer me a free ride. There was no way that my dad would be able to afford the tuition on his laborer's salary, so I couldn't go. It was a crushing blow, but I eventually got over it, encouraged by the fact that someone as respected as Mr. Beck thought I had the talent to go there.

Years later, I would become best known for my voice, but back in those days I had absolutely no interest in singing. I didn't take part in any school choirs or choruses, just orchestras and bands. I was quite content to be a drummer and a songwriter. Someone else could sing the songs.

Ben, who is about 3½ years older than me, chose to follow my father and play trumpet. And, unlike me with the drums, he was a natural the instant my dad showed him what to do and he began blowing into that horn. By the time Ben was in high school, he had formed his own band—the Blue Tones. They featured the sax, piano, bass guitar, and drums, and would focus on music by modern jazz artists like Dave Brubek and Thelonious Monk, who was a wicked piano player. The Blue Tones were so good that they took part in a battle of the bands at the old War Memorial Auditorium in Rochester. There were about 20 bands in the competition, and each was allowed to play three songs. Judges, often swayed by the audience's response, would determine which acts advanced. I think the Blue Tones finished in the top two, and that publicity helped them book jobs around town like nobody's business.

My younger brother, who was four years my junior, was a very bright kid—somewhat of an intellectual and an introvert.

He taught himself to play the guitar when he was 11 and, like Ben, it came to him naturally.

Dad always had his car radio tuned to jazz. He loved listening to Mel Torme, Harry James, Ella Fitzgerald, and the Dorsey Brothers. One day we were going someplace in his '53 Pontiac, and I guess he had his fill of music and started turning the dial in search of the news or a ballgame. He got distracted for a second, and the radio wound up on a pop music station. This DJ came on and said, "Now here's the latest from that up-and-coming recording artist, Elvis Presley. It's called 'Hound Dog,' and I think it's going to become a big hit." Ben and I were sitting in the backseat, and our ears perked up immediately. We got to listen to about 20 seconds of this rousing song before Dad, who was muttering under his breath, "What is this shit?" abruptly switched the station. All we had heard, essentially, were the opening lyrics—"You ain't nothing but a hound dog, cryin' all the time." But that's all we needed to hear. Ben and I had these looks of incredulity, like we had just discovered a hundred dollar bill on the sidewalk. That was my introduction to rock 'n' roll—Elvis' "Hound Dog" blasting out of the dashboard speakers of my Dad's '53 Pontiac. I didn't realize it at the time, but that would wind up being a life-altering experience. A whole new world was about to open up for me.

I can remember hanging with my older brother and some kids across the street, and we'd be singing harmonies to Dion and the Belmonts and stuff from that era. We knew all the words to all the songs by the Everly Brothers. Our parents and others in the neighborhood would watch us put on our little Doo-Wop concerts. I guess you could say that was my first involvement with a music group.

As I mentioned, we would spend Sundays at my grandparents' house, and after we consumed heaping plates of spaghetti and meatballs smothered in homemade sauce, we'd gather in the living room to listen to either *The Italian Hour* radio show or my grandfather playing the mandolin. Grampa was an excellent musician, but he couldn't carry a tune to save his life. That, however, didn't stop him from singing at the top of his lungs while playing the mandolin. It was funny at first, but then it became painful. One by one, we kids would discreetly disappear from the room during Grampa's concerts. Ben and I would usually wind up in the bedroom of our older cousin because she had this tiny little record player and a bunch of 45s that we would play and sing along to. I remember listening to artists like the Everly Brothers, Buddy Holly, Johnny Cash, Dion and the Belmonts, and Little Richard. One Sunday we were spinning tunes when she put on this new 45 she had just purchased, and I finally got a chance to listen to the entire version of "Hound Dog" and learn about this Elvis guy. I was absolutely mesmerized. The sound and the man behind it were so distinctive, so cool. I couldn't wait to hear and see more.

When Ben and I got home, we told our parents about how our cousin was allowed to have a rock 'n' roll record collection and how we wanted to be able to start our own collection. My parents adamantly refused. My dad grumbled, "You're not playing that garbage in our house. It's nothing but noise, and the lyrics are filthy." But that didn't stop us from continuing to bug them about it. Eventually, we wore them down and they relented. But we were told we could only play the records when they weren't home. Dad warned us that if he heard that "crap" being played in his presence, he'd grab the record off the turntable and break it into a million pieces.

Ben and I started buying records at Neisner's, a downtown Rochester department store where my mother worked. When we would go with Dad to pick her up, we would spend whatever money we could scrounge together on 45s. You could get them for 29 cents back in those days. I'll never forget buying the record "Louie, Louie" by The Kingsmen. There were other versions done later, but this was *the* original version, a true classic, and I swear I played that record so many times I wore out the grooves.

I was about 12 years old when I received one of the best gifts of my life—my first set of drums. They were actually used drums and about 25 years old, but I didn't care. In my mind, they were as good as new. My dad got them from my Uncle Phil, who used to play in big bands during the 1940s but hadn't picked up the sticks in years. They were Gretsch drums built in the 1930s, and they were really sharp-looking, painted in a blue lacquer with a touch of gold. They were enormous and took up so much space that we could barely fit them in Dad's car, which was as big as a tank. Once home, we set them up in our basement. I was so small and they were so big that I could barely reach the cymbals, but we arranged it so that it was just right for me.

It took me some time to become comfortable with the coordination needed to become a good drummer. People think you only need your hands. But in reality, you need both of your hands and both of your feet to operate in synch. The trick is that each hand and foot is doing something different at the same time, so it requires an awful lot of coordination. But I eventually got the hang of it and spent hours down there, playing everything from swing music to rock.

Like I said, I had the heights of my drums and the seat adjusted perfectly for me. But not long after my dad and I set things up, I began to notice that somebody had been using my drums without my knowledge. I'd go down to play and notice that the snare drum was 6" higher and I couldn't reach the cymbals. I naturally suspected that my brother, Ben, had been screwing around with things just to annoy me. He claimed innocence, but I knew better. One day, I told Ben I was going down the street to play ball with some friends. But after I walked out the door I went to the side of our house and peered through the basement window. Sure enough, within minutes, there was Ben in the cellar, adjusting everything on my drum set to suit him. Then he started playing, and my heart sank. As I listened to him bang away, I became demoralized because I realized that he was miles ahead of me, even though he had never taken a lesson and had not put in a fraction of the time I had. It just didn't seem fair, but the bottom line was that he was a natural and I wasn't. Of course, the resentment and envy has long since passed. Ben wound up becoming a very accomplished drummer, and I'm thrilled that he's now drumming for our band.

My poor mom had her hands full with us, especially during summers when we were off from school and more rambunctious than usual. Ben and I would constantly be at each other's throats, and she would have to come in like a boxing referee and separate us. Being several years older, Ben had more privileges than me, and that really bugged me. When Mom and Dad went out, they would take my younger brother with them and leave Ben in charge of me. One time he did something to really piss me off, and I decided to get back at him. I took three of his favorite 45-rpm records and hid them under this runner Mom had put down over the rug in a heavily trafficked area of the living room. I called Ben something to get him to run after me, and he came barreling across the runner. You could hear those vinyls crunching beneath his feet. He stopped to lift up the runner and when he saw the damage to his precious records, he was primed to kill me. I was smaller and faster, and I tore out the front door. He sprinted after me with every intention of strangling me. I raced around the house and through the front door and locked it so he couldn't get in. He was so incensed he broke a window and started climbing into the house just as my parents were pulling into the driveway. We were both in big, big trouble.

I remember another time when Mom took out this wooden spoon that her mother had given to her and she rapped Ben on the rear and broke the family heirloom. That just made her more livid. "Wait until your father gets home!" she screamed, repeating one of her common refrains. The minute Dad walked into the door, exhausted from a tough day at work, she gave him an earful about our latest transgressions. And Dad, who was usually mild-mannered, went over to the closet and pulled out his wide leather strap—just like the ones barbers used to sharpen razors—and gave us several whacks across the fanny. You'd think the welt on your backside would be a deterrent from further recalcitrant behavior, but it didn't stop Ben and me from having more brotherly spats. The older I got, the more I resented having to beg for mercy when Dad was applying the leather to my rear and turning my buttocks into raw hamburger.

We moved out to a new housing development in Gates, a suburb west of Rochester, when I was about 11 years old, and at first it was a real culture shock. It felt like we had gone from the city to the country. But I eventually adjusted to my new neighborhood and my new school, Gates Chili, which drew students from two different towns and had a much larger enrollment than I was used to in the city.

2

Banding Together

I blame the Rolling Stones for instigating my first and biggest act of parental defiance during my rebellious teenage years. It was November 1, 1965. I was 15 at the time, and my girlfriend—who was an absolute doll—told me that Mick Jagger and company were coming to town and that she had bought tickets for us. I was young and in love with her and rock 'n' roll, so this was clearly the best present anyone had ever given me. Yes, I was a huge Beatles fan, but I liked the Stones, too. During this time, Mick and his mates were just beginning to do the cutting-edge stuff that made them so distinctive. I couldn't wait to see them live with my squeeze.

But there was just one problem. When I asked my parents if I could go to the concert, they took about a nano-second to tell me, "Absolutely not!" They, like parents across the country, were aware of the Stones' bad-boy reputation. The band had been banned in certain cities because their raucous concerts often resulted in riotous behavior in which numerous kids were arrested. Ben and Nikki Grammatico were genuinely concerned for my safety. No matter what I said, I wasn't going to convince them to change their minds. "You're not going! End of discussion!" I was devastated but ultimately undeterred. *To hell with them*, I thought to myself, *I'm going*.

The other issue I had to deal with was my hair. I had one of those Beatles mop cuts, but it was too long in my father's eyes. He and I were always battling about that. When I was young I had no say in its length because he did the cutting himself—which meant a military brush cut. But I had reached an age where I was going to the barber. Invariably, I'd walk out of there and Dad wouldn't be pleased. "So Louis, which strand of hair did the barber cut today?" he'd ask sarcastically. And often he would drag me back into the barber's chair and have more lopped off. About a week before the concert, Dad told me it was time to get my ears lowered, as he liked to say, but I was deftly able to keep putting off the shearing. "I'll do it tomorrow, Dad. I'm too busy with school work, and this and that right now." Tomorrow would come and I'd offer up the same excuse. My goal was to hold out until after the Stones concert because there was no way I was going to show up there with some short, unhip do—especially when I was trying to impress my girl and fit in with the rest of the band's fans.

After supper the night of the concert, I went up to my room, put on my madras shirt, my tight jeans, and my British Walkers, dragged a comb through my hair, stashed the few bucks I had in my pocket, and plotted my escape. I knew the only way I was going to pull this off was to run as fast as I could down the stairs and through the front screen door. And that's what I did. I flew down the stairs and out of the house, the door slamming in my wake. By the time I had gotten about 10 houses down the street, I could hear my father screaming at the top of his lungs, "Louis! Louis! Get back here now!" I never looked back. I just kept motoring like an Olympic sprinter, fueled by both the fear of my father and the anticipation of being able to see the Stones.

Upon reaching the main drag to the city, I began hitchhiking and fortunately caught a ride with some other concert-goers. I met my girlfriend at a designated spot outside the War Memorial, and we herded into the building with thousands of others. The place was absolutely electric, and it was like an explosion the instant Mick and his boys started playing. The crowd was really into it—as it turned out, too much so. A couple of times, the show had to be stopped because fans—especially screaming teenage girls—were crushing one another, and a few unruly people jumped up onto the stage. About the third time this happened, Rochester Police Chief William Lombard had enough. He and several policemen came on stage after just the sixth or seventh song and grabbed the microphone from Jagger. "I had warned you people before that this needed to stop or else," he yelled into the microphone. "But you didn't listen, so this concert is officially over." Lombard said to reporters later that he decided to stop the show before the Stones got to what he called "the exhibitionist song" when Jagger stripped to his undershirt. The Chief never did give the name of the song, and to this day it remains a mystery.

Not surprisingly, his announcement was greeted with thunderous boos and some thrown objects. We all began chanting, "We want the Stones! We want the Stones!" All these years later, I can still see a rectangular pack of gum hurtling end over end through the air from the seats toward the stage. It wound up striking Detective Andrew Sparacino in the eye, and he lurched back as if he had been shot. His fellow officers caught him before he fell. It was a scary sight. I found out later that he almost lost his eye and wound up having vision problems the rest of his life. "It was our first experience here in dealing with rock concerts," Lombard told *Upstate* magazine in a 1985 retrospective. "I ordered the show stopped because things were getting out of hand, including the tempers of our officers. Some of them were literally being assaulted.... It was [very close to] becoming a real riot, in my judgment." Lombard went on to say that the Stones weren't very cooperative. "It was deliberately provoked; there was no question about it," he said. "That lead singer—what's his name?—would open up his shirt and throw things into the audience." I remember Lombard and Jagger getting into a little bit of a shoving match at one point, an incident which the police chief corroborated in that article twenty years later. "Oh, there was a little pushing, a little grabbing of the arm," Lombard said. "Nothing serious." After the plug was pulled on the show, guitarist Keith Richards didn't pull any punches, yelling to reporters, "This is a hick town. They were twice as wild in Montreal. They won't get hurt. You're too hard with them."

The Stones' reputation as surly louts who incited mayhem clearly had preceded them. Lombard and his staff were well aware that three of the band's members had been fined £5 each for "insulting behavior" after a show in Romford, England, in which they urinated against a gas station wall following the concert. And television host Ed Sullivan, whose prime-time variety hour was the most-watched show in America, vowed to ban them forever after their raucous appearance in the fall of 1964. "I promise you they'll never be back on our show," Sullivan told reporters. "I was shocked when I saw them. It took me 17 years to build this show. I'm not going to have it destroyed in a matter of weeks." As a result of this negative advance publicity, Rochester authorities braced themselves for the worst, employing a security force of 120—the largest that had ever been used for an event at the War Memorial.

After Lombard canceled the concert prematurely, about 25 Rochester policemen locked arms to prevent the frenzied fans from storming the stage. My girlfriend and I figured it was best to get out of the building because we feared things might get really ugly. We ran out a side door and, wouldn't you know it, the Stones' limo was right there and the musicians were being escorted into it. My girlfriend loved Brian Jones, and she broke through security and started screaming like a maniac, "Brian, I love you!" He brushed her off, got into the car, and she wound up jumping on the back trunk. The limo began to pull away, and she fell off and bumped her head against the street. They stopped the limo and Brian got out and helped her up and talked to her for about a minute while a cop checked out her bruised noggin. Jones then kissed her on the cheek and got back into the limo and it sped away.

We wound up going to a party some of her friends were throwing in a neighborhood several miles away on the other side of town. I was having a grand old time, and the next thing I know, I looked at my watch and it was a quarter after three in the morning. I was already in deep trouble, and I knew I had to get home before the sun came up or my father was going to kill me. My girlfriend and her friends scrounged up whatever change they could, and I called a cab. When the taxi pulled into my driveway, I counted up all my money and realized that I was about $2 short. I began pleading with the driver. "Look, the minute I walk into that door, I'm going to die. I'm so sorry, but

I don't have enough money to pay the fare. Here's everything I got." The guy wasn't pleased, but he could see that the fear on my face was genuine. "All right, kid," he growled. "Get the hell out of here."

The house was completely dark. I opened the door as quietly as I could and gingerly stepped inside. I took one step up the stairs when the lights flicked on. I nearly soiled my pants. My father was sitting in his living room chair. Fortunately, his barber's strap was nowhere to be seen. His voice was firm but not loud. "Louis, I don't know what got into you that would cause you to defy your mother and father like this. I'm very, very disappointed in you. You are grounded for a month. No outside activities after school or on the weekends. No nothing." "Yes, sir," I said. I headed up the stairs, and after I closed the door to my room, I pumped my fist and said, "All right!" For all that I had done, I didn't think the penalty was too severe. I thought for sure my father was going to get out the strap and tan my hide.

When I was with Foreigner 12 years later, we were invited by the Stones to play before them at a concert in front of 80,000 fans at old RFK Stadium in Philadelphia. They actually introduced us as "special guests of the Rolling Stones." That was so cool. And it prompted me to call home and say, "Hey Dad, remember that time you forbade me to go to the Stones concert? Well, I went again." We had a good chuckle over that one.

• • •

Like I said, I was a huge Beatles fan. No group before or since ever impacted me the way they did, and I know I have plenty of company when I say that because the Fab Four revolutionized music and the industry. Their songs were so distinctive, and it was amazing to watch their music evolve from simple love songs to complicated social commentaries along the way. But the Beatles' impact went beyond their music. They created a style—from their perfectly coiffed mop-top haircuts when they first started out to their unruly beards and long hair toward the end—that influenced everything from hairstyles to clothes. They created an image, a persona. We came to know their personalities as if they were close friends or members of the family.

There were certainly other bands I enjoyed during the first and second British Invasion—Free, The Animals, Traffic, Humble Pie, and the Kinks among them—but none of them reached the level of the Beatles. I'll never forget watching them live on *The Ed Sullivan Show* during their first trip to America. You could feel the excitement coming through our little black-and-white television screen. I remember stealing a glance at my mom and dad that night, and I noticed them smirking. My dad shook his head, his disdain obvious. His attitude was that this was a bunch of noise with no lasting value, just a fad that would soon fade away. But as the show went on, I saw my mother getting into one of the love songs sung by Lennon and McCartney. And that pissed off my father. He looked at Mom as if she were some sort of traitor. To his credit, Dad wound up giving the Beatles a chance, and after a few years he came around and realized that these guys weren't flashes in the pan but brilliant, influential musicians whose work would stand the test of time.

At the height of the Beatles' popularity, people would take sides about who they liked best: Lennon or McCartney. I liked them both, but Lennon was more my guy because there was more of an edge and attitude to his music, and I always liked that in a musician. It didn't have to be perfect to be good, and Lennon understood that sometimes the imperfections and the rawness were what made a song stand out.

Back around 1972 after my group, Black Sheep, had signed a deal with Capitol Records, I had a chance meeting with my hero. We were recording at the studios they used in New York, and during a break I walked into the lounge to clear my head and grab a cappuccino. Well lo and behold, there was Lennon, who had been recording in one of the nearby studios. It was just me and him in this rec room, and I was shocked when he introduced himself and began chatting with me. Maybe the biggest shock was that I was actually able to speak. He asked me what studio I was in and a little bit about our band and the type of music we played. He was working on an album at the time with Phil Spector, and he talked about how this particular album was a vast departure from the albums he had produced with the Beatles. I recall him being very healthy looking—I believe this was after he had sought some help to get off the alcohol and the drugs. I don't recall him offering any words of encouragement, other than to say that first and second albums were very tough because it took time for a band to find out who they were and develop an identity. He was friendly but somewhat reserved. He did ask me if I wanted to play a game of pool, and I said, "Sure." I discovered right away that he was pretty good. He beat me soundly and then excused himself to get back to work. In retrospect I wish I had a camera with me. I would have loved to have had my picture taken with him. Then again, who needs a photograph? The memory of the moment is indelible.

Every die-hard John Lennon fan remembers where he or she was the night of December 8, 1980, when Lennon was murdered by John David Chapman. I was just five blocks away in our recording studio, laying down tracks for Foreigner's 4 album. As I drove home to Westchester that night, I went past the Dakota where John and Yoko Ono lived, and I saw the crowds of people that had gathered for a candlelight vigil. They were singing Lennon songs and holding candles. I shed a few tears on my ride home that night.

A decade after Lennon was murdered, I was one of the dozen or so artists asked to perform in a tribute concert from the docks in Liverpool, not far from where the legendary Beatle grew up. It was a tremendous honor for me to be able to pay tribute to one of my music idols and to do so with the likes of B.B. King, Roberta Flack, Al Green, Sarah Vaughan, Joe Cocker, and Randy Travis. The promoters assembled a band of world-class session players, and each performer sang a different Lennon tune. I wound up doing about three songs, including "Eight Days a Week." I could feel John's presence all around. I walked the streets a little bit, and one of the highlights was peeking inside The Cavern Club where the Beatles cut their teeth—now it's like a museum.

I never met George Harrison, but I did meet the other two Beatles. When I was with Foreigner, we had backstage passes for a Paul McCartney concert at Madison Square Garden, and when the show ended we were able to meet him and chat a bit. I met Ringo Starr when his All-Star band made a summer tour stop in Canandaigua, near Rochester. I was there to see my friend Nils Lofgren, who was a guitarist in the band and had been gracious enough to play several tracks on my solo hit, "Midnight Blue." Nils must have told Ringo I was there because he wound up calling me onto the stage and had me sing a song. It caught me totally off-guard, but I went up there and belted out something for him.

One other Beatles moment for me occurred in 2008 when rock pioneer and longtime Ringo friend Todd Rundgren asked me to join an All-Star cast for a live performance celebrating the 40th anniversary of the Beatles' release of the Sgt. Pepper album. Other artists included former Wings member Denny Laine, *American Idol* winner Bo Bice, and Grammy Award winner Christopher Cross. The show, which raised money for prostate cancer research, was produced by Geoff Emerick, the original engineer for the Sgt. Pepper album. It was very special.

The other English groups I really loved were Humble Pie and Free. In my mind, they were the epitome of hard rockers, and I absolutely loved their intensity. In the early 1970s, I remember seeing Humble Pie in concert three straight nights—Buffalo, Rochester, and Syracuse. I also remember cramming into a Volkswagen with some buddies and driving to New York to see Free open for Dr. Hook and the Edgar Winter Group. I loved Free's lead singer Paul Rodgers and guitarist Paul Kossoff. Their signature song was "All Right Now," and I vividly remember them belting that out during a 40-minute performance that was as mesmerizing as any concert I've ever witnessed. Even though it was an uncomfortable trip being crammed in that little bug, I'm so happy I had a chance to see Free live because shortly after that the band disbanded and Kossoff died of a drug-induced heart attack.

Musically, I also was deeply influenced by several Motown artists, including Marvin Gaye and Aretha Franklin. While with Foreigner I was able to perform in an anniversary concert for Atlantic Records that included Aretha. That was a great thrill. Every singer influences you in different ways. And when I look back at those recording artists from Detroit, I realize that people like Marvin and Aretha taught me the importance of singing not only with your vocal chords but with your soul.

• • •

My first paying gig came when I was just 15 years old. I got a call from a guy named Tony, who said their drummer had broken his arm and someone had recommended me to them. I had never played with any bands, so I think the recommendation may have come from someone in my brother's group. I would be filling in for a country-and-western band known as Donny, Tony & the Knighthawks, and they would be playing at PJ's Bar and Lounge on West Avenue, which at the time was the C&W hotspot in Rochester. I got thrown into the deep end of the pool because my first time playing with them would be a show.

To say I was nervous would be an understatement. I was crapping my pants. Here I was 15 years old, never having played any of these songs before with a bunch of guys in their early forties in front of a rowdy crowd of about 120 people who were enjoying their beer. (Which, in hindsight, might have been a good thing from my perspective; the tipsier the audience, the less they would notice any flubs by me.) Before each song, either Donny or Tony would turn to me and tell me what the beat was supposed to be. I took it from there, keeping up the rhythm until they signaled to me that the song was coming to an end. A couple of times, Donny and Tony would tell the audience that I was filling in for so-and-so and, "For not knowing the songs, he's doing a heck of a job, ain't he?" The crowd was quite forgiving—not to mention feeling no pain—and I was serenaded with loud, encouraging applause.

We wound up playing three 40-minute sets, and when it was over, they paid me about $40. Dad could see the sparkle in my eye as he helped me break down my drum set and load it into his car. I wound up playing about a dozen shows with the Knighthawks, and when their drummer was healthy enough to return, they thanked me profusely for tiding them over. Although country wasn't my thing, it was a cool experience and I'll always be grateful to them for giving me the opportunity to feel what it was like to play a gig in front of a crowd.

My role as a fill-in drummer whetted my appetite for being in a band full-time. And I took steps to sate that appetite when I was a sophomore in high school, around 1966. They had fraternities in high schools back then, and one of my frat brothers played the guitar. To be honest, he wasn't very good, but he had good equipment and he said he knew this older bass player who might be interested in jamming with us. The guy's name was Butch, and he was something like 27 years old and had slicked-back hair with an Elvis doodle in the front. When I first met him I immediately asked myself what I was doing playing with this guy—he's going to be more into Doo-Wop. But the three of us started jamming, and I felt the magic right away.

After a few sessions, we added a rhythm player and started working on a repertoire of songs. We learned several songs by the Stones and Beatles, as well as some Ray Charles stuff and the Animals classic, "House of the Rising Sun." It was a pretty good mix. Then we shopped ourselves around and landed our first gig at the Chili Grange. It was this big, old room next door to a graveyard that held about 200 to 300 kids, and they had booked three bands that night. In between band sets, I remember kids heading out to the cemetery to make out. The headliner was set up on the stage, while we set up on the floor off to the side in one of the corners. It stunk not being on the stage because you really couldn't see much of the crowd, and I remember the acoustics being terrible—incredible echoes—a really tough place to play. But I didn't care. I was in my own band, and it was fantastic.

We called ourselves PHFTT, which didn't stand for anything but was so distinctive that people remembered it. I was the lead singer as well as the drummer, and I found it difficult to do both at first. As I mentioned earlier, it takes a lot of coordination just to play the drums because you have four appendages (your hands and your feet) that have to be in synch. Then when you add in the vocals, it becomes even more challenging. There would be some songs where I'd be really winded by the end. But I eventually got the hang of it, and it became second nature.

We played about a dozen shows, including a few more at the Grange hall and some local high schools. But the group only lasted for about a year before going, well, PHFTT. Our rhythm player wound up quitting, and our lead guitar player went off to college. The bass player and I became pretty good friends, and we went out and found a singer, a guitar player, and an organ player and formed a new band that we called the St. James Infirmary.

Joe Gallo, the organ player, was a high school classmate of mine. He and I would get together after school at his house and screw around writing songs. Joe also came from a musical family—his dad was a very good tenor sax player. Joe and I got so into songwriting that we decided there wasn't enough time after school to do it and our homework, so we began carving out time during school, as well. We were in gym together and when it was time to go outside, we'd sneak off and run to his house, which was nearby, and work on our songs for about a half hour.

After a while, we started skipping school on occasion and would go over to the house of a mutual friend, Tony Gaudio, to fine-tune our songs. Tony's mom didn't have a problem with it because we didn't do it that often and she saw how passionate we were about our music. She viewed these as jam sessions rather than us playing hooky. She would brew a pot of coffee for us and serve as a sounding board while we experimented with our songs on the piano. Ma Gaudio would be very encouraging. She'd say things like, "Oh, I really like that one. That song has a lot of potential." She became our biggest fan. Ma Gaudio believed so deeply in us that she occasionally would call in sick for us so we didn't get into trouble with our parents and could spend an entire day working on our music. We'd head to her house instead of the bus stop in the morning, and she'd phone the school nurse. "Hi, this is Mrs. Gaudio. Joey's not feeling well today, I'm going to keep him home." Then about five minutes later, she would call the nurse's office again and say, "Hi, this is Mrs. Grammatico. Louis isn't feeling well today." The nurse eventually caught on because one time after Ma called in for me, the nurse said, "Thank you, Mrs. Gaudio."

Initially, I played drums and sang backup for the Infirmary. Our lead vocalist was a guy named Tom Regna, who had a voice that sounded like Eric Burdon, the front man from the 1960s British band, The Animals. Not surprisingly, we took advantage of that vocal similarity and played a lot of Animals songs during our gigs. Tom's house on 126 Matilda Street in Rochester was our studio, so to speak. When the weather was cold, we'd practice in the basement, and when it was warm, we'd rehearse in the garage. I vividly remember how Tom's dad had an old player-piano in the basement, and when we finished playing we'd dig into this big box of piano rolls—they were about as big as a cardboard toilet-paper roll—and insert them into the piano and it would start playing songs.

Our garage rehearsals during the summer months received mixed reviews from the neighbors. About a dozen kids who lived on Matilda would gather at the end of the Regna's driveway and listen to us with these curious looks on their faces. The adult neighbors were more angry than curious. Between songs they'd be yelling at us to turn down the volume. There were a few occasions when the police showed up and threatened to arrest us and confiscate our instruments if we didn't stop violating the city's noise ordinance, which went into effect around 8:00 PM. Such were the risks of being in a garage band.

I was about 17 at the time and had definitely reached a stage in my life where I was totally obsessed with rock music. I would sit in class and draw drum sets and guitars. And I would make up names of bands and scrawl them on the face of the drums, a la the Beatles. If I was really bored, I would start making a list of song names for an imaginary album.

I don't remember the first song I ever wrote, but I do remember us being somewhat unique just by attempting to come up with some original stuff. Back then virtually every group in Rochester was a cover band. And for the most part we were, too. We were covering Top 40 songs from the radio, but our desire was to slip in one of our own songs here and there. To be honest, I don't remember any of the Infirmary's originals being very good, but we were at least giving it a try. The band lasted for a few years before breaking up. I think I was a freshman at Monroe Community College when we disbanded, and I was still wondering what I was going to do with my life. Although it had been fun doing the gigs with PHFTT and The St. James Infirmary, I hadn't experienced the kind of success that would lead me to believe that I could make a living as a full-time musician. And on those rare occasions when I believed otherwise, Dad would soberly remind me that music was a good avocation but not a good vocation.

My parents emphasized the importance of education and I was—when I applied myself—a very good student. I loved art and music, but I was also a big history buff. I was intrigued by American history, especially the Revolutionary and Civil War eras, and I liked reading about our presidents. One of the big thrills of my youth was being able to see presidential candidate John F. Kennedy pass by us in a convertible during a 1960 campaign stop in Rochester. If I hadn't pursued a career in rock 'n' roll, I definitely would have become a history teacher. In fact, after graduating from Gates Chili High School in 1968, that's what I majored in at Monroe Community College—education and art. But my heart was more into my music and my bands than my studies, which is why I joke that I spent four years matriculating at a two-year college.

After the demise of The St. James Infirmary, I joined an established band called Poor Heart. They played fairly steadily, and I figured I'd just enjoy myself and make a little extra money on the side. The interesting thing is that I joined them not as a drummer but as a singer. They were already committed to their drummer, but they needed another voice. They were kind of structured after Three Dog Night, essentially a rock band and three vocalists. I hit it off right away with the other two singers— Barry Middleton and Joe Pullaro. We harmonized well together, and the band became very successful. We were so good that our manager got us invited to a recording studio in San Francisco to cut an album at no expense to us. We had written quite a few songs to that point, but we were naïve to the ways of the music business. We wound up signing away the rights to the songs to the man who owned the studio and was going to produce the album. The idea was to record the album, and they would try to sell it to a label. We spent about a month there and recorded 11 or 12 songs. It was a great experience and, looking back, I realize it was another step in my progression as a musician.

We returned home with a flicker of hope that we were about to catch our first big break. As it turned out, the album went nowhere. The guy didn't even give us a demo copy. We couldn't help but feel a little bitter. In retrospect, I can say that was my first experience with the not-always-pleasant business side of the music industry. I would experience far worse shenanigans down the road.

Interestingly, years later, when I started enjoying success with Foreigner, the Poor Heart songs we recorded finally surfaced in a bootleg album that was titled *Lou Gramm: The Early Years*. They titled the album after me even though I was the lead singer on only three of the nine songs and it really was a Poor Heart album, not a Lou Gramm album. The finished product they put together was pretty amateurish. They cut out a picture of my head from Foreigner's *Double Vision* album and superimposed it on the cover of the bootleg album. And there was no mention of Poor Heart. They were obviously trying to capitalize on my success although they didn't have the legal rights to bill it the way they did. Fortunately, none of the songs were ever played on the radio, but they did make a few bucks selling it underground. It was later repackaged and resurfaced in Europe.

Listening to those songs today, I realize they were just so-so. Our harmonizing was very good, our voices quite strong, but the reality was that we were young songwriters in the very early stages of our careers and the album reflected that. We worked hard, but we just weren't ready or deserving of an album. I spent about a year-and-a-half to two years with Poor Heart, and we developed a solid following in Rochester, Syracuse, and Buffalo. We were booked virtually every weekend, and the money wasn't bad, especially for a college student. We'd get about $450-$500 a night, while most local groups were getting $250-$300.

After returning from our recording session in San Francisco, I played a few more shows with Poor Heart, but I felt this pull to do something more. The bug to record my own music had bitten me. I was beginning to form my own concepts for songs and what a band should sound like. I wanted to do more rock that had a swagger and was tinged with blues. Although I was grateful that Poor Heart had pursued me after The St. James Infirmary folded, I was thinking the time might be right to break away and start anew. The guys in Poor Heart understood. There weren't any hard feelings. They stayed together for another year or two, and I'm still friends with the original members. I think they knew when they brought me on board that I was really just passing through.

3

The Black Sheep of Rock

Like me, Larry Crozier had grown tired of playing Top 40 songs for Poor Heart and wanted to form a group that played album cuts you didn't hear on the AM radio dial—as well as music we created. So when I told him of my plans for starting a new band, he asked if he could join me. And I was more than happy to have him aboard because Larry was a talented keyboard player. He was also well plugged in to the local music scene, so he'd be able to help me find the musicians we needed to make this thing fly. We immediately recruited my younger brother, a guitarist, and then added Bruce Turgon, who would become our bass player and collaborate with me on writing the majority of the songs. Other early members of the band that would become known as Black Sheep included Tom Fire, a musician from Buffalo, and Ron Rocco, who hailed from Rochester. During the band's formative years, we went through several personnel changes. Down the road, we convinced a promising young guitar player named Don Mancuso to join the lineup. Donnie has been a lifelong friend and still plays in my band today. Back then, though, he was so young and raw. I think we literally pulled him out of high school to play for us.

In our early days, we would play songs like "All Right Now" by Free and "Feeling All Right" by Joe Cocker. We'd also perform a couple of tunes that were kind of bluesy, then we'd do some Traffic before toughening it up with some Humble Pie. I guess you could say we rocked hard, but our chords were steeped in the blues. During shows we'd slide in an original or two, which wasn't common for local bands to do. My game plan was for us to eventually stage shows where two-thirds of the stuff we played was our own. One critic described Black Sheep as "an Anglophilic hard rock band." I liked that description because we had been profoundly influenced by the British invasions.

I had been inspired by a number of Rochester bands over the years—the Showstoppers, Brass Buttons, Lincoln Zephyr, and the Red, White & Blues Band—groups that had written their own stuff and had stood out from the crowd. That's what I envisioned for us. We didn't want to be just a cover band; we wanted to be distinctive, carve our own niche. And my dream was to eventually land us a record contract, cut an album, and expand our audience beyond upstate New York.

It was a huge struggle at first; it always is when you're a new band. But it was more so for us because we were trying to create a sound that was all our own at a time when club owners and a lot of fans expected local groups to stick to covering the national acts. We really had to hustle. Initially, we would play any gig we could get, no matter how small the venue. That meant doing high school dances and town halls just to get the exposure. Eventually, people took notice and word of mouth spread about our hot new group, and we started booking gigs in popular Rochester-area rock clubs such as the Orange Monkey, the Brass Rail, and the Penny Arcade. We received a nice publicity boost early on when music critic Jack Garner reviewed one of our club performances in the *Rochester Times-Union* newspaper on July 22, 1971:

"Black Sheep is an apropos name because their approach to music is a little different from the rest of the flock. For one thing there's no show to this band. They just sit or stand at their respective instruments and play good music. No dramatics, no clowning, no tricks—just music.

"Secondly, they don't play your everyday AM radio Top 40. Instead, they get into virtually unknown album cuts, and obscure things from people like Spooky Tooth and Dave Mason. It will be the rare night that you hear many familiar songs. They'd rather appeal to listeners who want new experiences. If you want to hear local versions of the song you heard on the car radio on the way to the concert, you might as well go back to the car radio."

Jack was taken by my percussionist skills, writing:

"When the band is on stage, your eyes are drawn to the thick-necked, perspiring drummer. He plays in a hard, steady, driving style, and works well with the cymbals. His changes are tasteful and interesting, and his tempos are letter-perfect."

He concluded his column with the kind of endorsement our band needed:

"Black Sheep are an interesting experience. They're not any sort of super-band with super-theatrics and willy-nilly, sing-along music. They'd rather just play stimulating and different and sometimes unknown music. It's dangerous to be different in the very commercial business of pop music.

"For that alone, they deserve some credit...and a listen."

Not long after that review, we also began performing in Buffalo clubs such as McVan's, and it was there in 1972 that we met Jim Taylor, who became our promotions manager. Jim had worked for A&M Records, a company that represented Humble Pie, Traffic, and Free, so it was a good fit for us and our style of music. Jim knew the business side of the industry and the things we needed to do to get our shot. He convinced us that it was about more than just the music, that the successful bands each had their own style, and that included the way they dressed. Of his own volition and on his own dime, he went out and bought these three-button suits like the ones that Rod Stewart wore, along with black velvet bell-bottom pants and some sharp-looking boots. He spent a lot of money on us, and it made us feel like he really believed in us.

The name Black Sheep came out of a bitch session we were having one day during a break from rehearsing. I was bemoaning the fact that Rochester club owners weren't giving us a chance. I said, "We're the black sheep of the music scene in this town," and Jim immediately picked up on that. He said, "That's what you should call yourselves. Use it as motivation." And that's what we did.

As a result of our desire to play deep album cuts and our own stuff, we wound up being ostracized. The clubs back then were partial to cover bands. They felt that audiences only wanted a rehash of the Top 40 songs they heard all day on the radio. We wanted to offer something different, but we knew in order to get our foot in the door, we'd have to play the game, so to speak. The club owners would ask us, "Do you play this song?" And we would tell them, "Oh, yeah. We can do that one." And they'd ask, "Well, what about that one?" And we'd tell them, "Yes, that one, too." And then we'd get the gig and we'd play some of those bands' more obscure album cuts, ones that hadn't made mainstream radio or the Billboard charts. And of course we slipped in our own stuff. We were outlaws who were willing to be different. Some people really appreciated that, and some didn't. Some clubs wouldn't ask us back because we weren't doing enough dance stuff, and that was fine with us.

One of those clubs that didn't ask us back was the Orange Monkey. Just before we started playing, everyone crowded onto the dance floor and sat down as if they were at a concert instead of a club. We put on a great performance that night, really killed it, and the people who sat instead of danced really appreciated our efforts. So afterward, we were feeling pretty good about ourselves. We went up to the manager and said, "Wasn't that great? Did you see how much the people were into our performance?" And he said, "That sucked. The more people dance, the more alcohol I serve and the more money I make. The less people dance, the less alcohol I sell and the less money I make. Here's your money for the night, and I guarantee you you'll never be asked to play here again. Pack up your stuff and get the hell out of here."

We were a little peeved at first but quickly shook it off. Hey, we weren't everyone's cup of tea, and we didn't want to be. We refused to compromise ourselves or our music, and that desire to be our own musicians and not play Top 40 stuff cost us a lot of money. But over time we developed a really loyal hardcore following. The word got out that we weren't like the other bands, and that's exactly what we wanted.

Jim Taylor wanted us to expand our reach beyond western New York and he got us some gigs in the New York City area. One of the venues included a concert at the Danbury (Connecticut) State Prison, which was a minimum-security jail that actually featured some of the guys involved in the Watergate break-in. Needless to say it was a pretty strange place to put on a concert. Here we are, on stage, all duded up in our fancy clothes, playing these sexy, provocative songs. About halfway through the concert it finally hit me like a ton of bricks that we're performing this stuff in front of 150 guys who probably hadn't been with a woman in quite some time. I immediately started toning things down. The second half of that concert was pretty bland, and I was just happy we got out of there without causing an uprising.

At Jim's urging, a friend of his from Capitol Records attended one of our gigs, and that got us stoked. Jim told us the guy was impressed—but apparently not impressed enough to want to sign us. Undaunted, we kept plugging along and caught a big break in the early 1970s when Jim landed us a deal to open for Procol Harum at their shows in Syracuse and Rochester. The road manager for Procol was Derek Sutton, who was a partner with Chrysalis Records, a hugely successful European label that represented artists such as Jethro Tull and Cat Stevens. Chrysalis was about to lease office space in New York and Chicago and was looking for an American band to promote. Sutton really liked the show we put on, and the next thing we knew we were signing a contract to become Chrysalis' first American act. The game plan called for us to produce a song they could heavily promote and market here in the States, and that would be followed by a few more singles and an album. We were ecstatic. All our hard work had finally paid off. I couldn't help but think about the club owners who had thrown us out because they didn't think our stuff was any good and wanted us to stick to playing other people's music. Vindication was sweet.

We already had several songs written, and Chrysalis decided to kick things off with "Stick Around." I totally agreed. It was a pretty cool, simplistic song with catchy lyrics that would stick in people's heads. It featured a memorable riff by Don Mancuso, who had replaced my brother as our lead guitarist. We went to the Record Plant in New York City to record it. And when we had finished I began counting the days until its release. I thought about that first time I had heard Elvis singing "Hound Dog" on my father's car radio. It was going to be so cool, listening to my voice and my band blasting through the dashboard of a car radio.

Well, dreams don't always unfold the way you want them to. The single came out and was played on radio stations in the Northeast and Midwest. People went to record stores in hopes of purchasing it and the album it was from, but there was no album and in many instances even the single wasn't available. We were feverishly working on other songs for an album, but as it turned out, Chrysalis' grandiose plans for making a splash with an American band in the U.S. went kaput. I think some of their European bands had jumped ship and they were having some financial problems, so our record never received the promotional push we had been promised and they weren't going to follow through on producing our album. It was a huge downer for us, a crushing blow. On Jim Taylor's advice, we quietly negotiated our release from Chrysalis. We didn't want the press to know because we would have been dismissed as just another band that had dreamed big but couldn't deliver. Jim arranged for us to resume opening for Procol Harum. And we continued to write more songs so that we would be ready to produce an album if another record label called.

Jim—God bless him—truly believed in us and kept hustling to find us work beyond Rochester. He lined up shows in some

Ohio theaters where we played with Ted Nugent, and in Kansas City where we opened for the Climax Blues Band. In a way, Jim was like us. He was hungry to make a name for himself, just like we were. We shared a common dream and a common goal.

By 1973, we had built a pretty good catalog of songs. It was just a matter of convincing someone to take a chance on us and make good on the promises that Chrysalis had failed to keep. Jim's persistence and perseverance finally bore fruit for us later that year after he convinced the executives at Capitol Records to give us an audition. I think we were better prepared to make our pitch this time around. Our songs were more refined, and we had developed a more definitive identity. Although they didn't like some of the stuff we played—and told us as much—they liked enough of our songs to believe we were ready to record an album and they offered us a two-album contract, which I'm told was unusual for startup groups in those days. Capitol picked the song "Chain on Me" to promote our first album, and I was happy with their choice because I felt it epitomized who we were and what we were about.

Another person who was really high on us was Stuart Alan Love, who had been a producer for Columbia records and had worked with the likes of Jethro Tull, James Taylor, and Earth, Wind & Fire. He thought so much of us that he left his job at Columbia to become our producer. He said he became smitten with our music the first time he heard us play in the summer of 1973. "Their rock songs were good, but in my mind, anybody can write a rock song," Love later told a reporter. "To me, it's the ballad that sets a group apart, and as soon as I heard one of their ballads, I was hooked. I had my secretary get me a plane to Rochester. I didn't want to give them to Columbia—they'd be just one of 50 million groups there." He wound up running the sound board controls for our concerts and recording sessions at the Record Plant studios and for rehearsals in a dilapidated barn in a rural area west of Rochester that belonged to Bruce Turgon.

Although the Capitol deal was a generous one, we were still struggling financially. Much of the money we received from them we spent on equipment and travel. Each of us was forced to continue to live in our parents' homes to make ends meet.

Stuart and Jim arranged for us to open for Ten Years After, a rowdy British blues-rock band whose hits included "Can You Hear Me Calling?" We were grateful for the opening gig, but we immediately discovered that touring isn't always what it's cracked up to be. Ten Years After had its own spacious plane with sofas and a flight attendant and unlimited food and drink. Meanwhile, we traveled from gig to gig in Jim's '73 Ford Galaxie. There was plenty of room in Jim's car, but it wasn't that comfortable when you were on the road for several hundred miles at a time.

There was one occasion when we played in Miami and had to be in Michigan two nights later. Fortunately, we didn't try to drive straight through. We stopped at a motor lodge in West Virginia that first morning to break up the trip. It seemed like an okay place, but it did have a few strange features. Each room had a speaker in it, and I remember the guy at the front desk kept playing this scratchy James Brown record. There was only one little lamp in my room, and I looked for a way to shut the speaker off. I finally realized that there was no switch on the speaker, so I wound up pulling the wires off it so I could get some sleep. When I woke up later that morning and opened the blinds to let some light in, I noticed that I had been sleeping in some filthy sheets. I was skeeved by that and immediately took a shower—of course, the hot water wasn't working. When we piled into Jim's tank to resume our trip to Michigan, each of us began sharing stories about the speakers and dirty sheets in each of our rooms. It dawned on us that this motor lodge was one of these places where guys paid $10 for a room, did their deed with a lady of the night, and took off. It was really disgusting. Not exactly the five-diamond hotel that Ten Years After and other main acts were used to. But such was life in the bush leagues of rock 'n' roll. It was part of the dues-paying process that every fledgling band experienced.

In retrospect, that tour did wonders for building our confidence. One of our final stops was in Chicago, where we were going to play in front of 20,000 people. I'll never forget arriving in the Windy City and running into some smart-assed teenagers who told me that the last three lead-off groups who performed there had been booed off the stage. One of the groups was the Raspberries. Another was the Electric Light Orchestra. Neither those negative comments nor the fact that some of our equipment had been lost bothered me or my band mates. We were ready to bring down the house—even if it meant performing in front of a skeptical audience and playing through rented amps. We absolutely nailed our songs that night, and we received rousing ovations and performed a couple of encores.

• • •

Our self-titled first album was released in 1974 and received some positive early reviews.

"If some of this sounds familiar, you're right," read one of them. "This is the closest sounding thing to Bad Company since the last Bad Company album. Vocalist Louie Grammatico sounds remarkably like Paul Rodgers in spots, while guitarist Donald Mancuso has mastered Mick Ralph's style. Still, the band is highly listenable on its own and is one of the better examples of the back-to-basics notion that seems strong in rock now. Material is generally strong and FM play should be strong. And don't discount a hit single from this package."

A critic for *Song & Dance*, at the time one of the music industry's top trade publications, wrote:

"If you like your roll buttered with the finest of rock, you'll dig the new Capitol Black Sheep LP. Messers Grammatico, Turgon, Crozier, Mancuso and Rocco have their act together and every track on the LP surges with energy and power."

Unfortunately, despite the encouraging words, neither our single nor our self-titled first album did very well. One of the problems was a lack of promotion. We were disappointed about that; we were expecting a lot more from a major record company that had accomplished so much. But we eventually came to the realization that we were the low men on the totem pole and that we were going to have to pay our dues and work even harder in order to convince Capitol to promote us more vigorously.

Our second album, *Encouraging Words*, came out in 1975 and it was much more polished. You could tell we were more focused, the songs held up better, and there was an identity, stylistically, that the first album lacked. We started getting some radio play time and some decent reviews after its release, but the thing we were most excited about—and the thing we believed that was going to truly launch us—was the news that we were going to be the opening act for KISS, which was at the height of its popularity with chart-toppers such as its signature song, "Rock and Roll All Night," dominating the airwaves. Tours were the best way to market your albums in those days. In fact, they were a must. And the fact that Capitol had paired us with KISS showed us that they had faith that we were a band of great potential. We were ecstatic and planned to grab onto KISS's coattails and generate the type of publicity that would enable us to one day, hopefully in the not-so-distant future, become a main act.

Stuart Alan Love's enthusiasm and belief in us was off the charts by this time. Before our tour commenced, he told a reporter, "It's my belief that we can make Black Sheep the No. 1 American act in the country." His optimism was echoed by Bob Buziak, an executive with Capitol, who told a reporter, "We're very excited about them.... Of our newer acts, we're most excited about them. Their chances of making it are excellent...in the upper 25 percent. They have excellent material; they put on an excellent show; they're a unique, fresh sound."

The first leg of the tour opened in Boston on Christmas Eve 1975 in the Orpheum Theater, a quaint 19th-century music hall featuring two balconies that were so close it felt as if you could reach out and shake hands with the people seated there. The curtain opened, there was an explosion of applause, and we began blasting away. Within a few notes, my nervousness disappeared and I was as calm as I had been as a young teenager, pounding away on my drums in my basement back in Gates. We played for about 40 minutes, and the audience was singing along with us, which made us feel fantastic because it meant that they were familiar with our second album, which had been receiving good air play. After playing our last song, we bowed and headed off the stage, but the applause wouldn't stop. We thought it was just the people being excited for the appearance of KISS, but they actually were jacked about us. Jim Taylor walked over to KISS's manager and asked him if it would be okay if we went out and did an encore. He said, "Sure." Ninety-nine percent of the time, this doesn't happen. When the opening act is done, it is done. Your job is to warm up the crowd. But we literally had touched a chord with that audience, so back out we went.

Once finished, there was more thunderous applause and we left the stage. The people were still going crazy so, with KISS's blessing, we went back and played a second encore. After we finished that song, we came off the stage for good, feeling like a million dollars. We got cleaned up, watched KISS perform, then piled into Jim's Ford Galaxie and drove back to Rochester, every mile reliving what had been the greatest night of our lives.

I got back to my apartment at about 4:00 AM and fell quickly into a deep sleep. About an hour later, I was roused awake by the phone. On the other end of the line was our crew chief, Steve Nider, and he sounded frantic. He told me that our equipment truck had hit an icy patch on the Thruway just west of Albany. "Is everybody okay?" I asked, my heart pounding through my chest. "Yes," he said, "just some bumps and bruises. But the truck is so mangled we can't even get the door open." A tow truck had managed to pull the wreckage to a nearby service station, but it was closed. I told him to wait there, that I would come with another band member to pick them up so they could get home and spend Christmas with their families. And that's what we did.

Two of us wound up spending Christmas day in Albany at that service station, assessing the damage. After prying at it for an hour with a crow bar, we finally managed to get the door open and were shocked to see that most of our equipment—the Hammond organ, the amplifiers, the speakers, and the drum shells—had been crushed. Our next show was scheduled for Cleveland on the 27th, so we were in a huge quandary. I couldn't get in touch with anyone from the insurance company until the morning after Christmas, and they didn't seem to share my sense of urgency about the need to get new equipment and a new truck immediately. We were a new band without much money so we didn't have the cash to go out and buy the stuff we needed.

Desperate, each of us approached our parents for money, but they were working-class people trying to make ends meet during a painful recession. They didn't have the means to bail us out.

After exhausting every possible solution, I called KISS's manager and told him about our dilemma in hopes that maybe we could borrow some equipment. He told me he was sorry about the accident but the show must go on. And as it turned out, it would go on without us. They scrambled to find another band, and we were dropped from the tour. About a week or two later, just when I thought things couldn't possibly get any worse, I received a call from Capitol Records that our record deal was being terminated. Emotionally, I was as mangled as our totaled equipment truck. I slammed down the phone as hard as I could and cursed at the top of my lungs. I then collapsed into a chair and began bawling uncontrollably. We had come oh-so-close to breaking through. We were on the verge. And just like that, it was all gone.

The insurance check finally arrived in April, and we went out and bought some new equipment. We would get together from time to time and talk about what was and what could have been. The conversation eventually would get around to how we should record some new songs and start playing the local clubs again. But each of us knew deep down that wasn't going to happen. As much as we didn't want to admit it, the band wasn't dormant, it was dead. We all had bills to pay, and each of us was trying to get on with his life.

The recession was raging around this time, and it was extremely difficult finding a job. Valenti's, the furniture store I had worked at since age 16, was hurting and could only give me one day a week. So I wound up going on welfare for a while. Three nights a week—from 6:00 PM to 11:00 PM—about 35 of us would be assigned to clean the judges' chambers at the Monroe County Public Safety Building in downtown Rochester. While I was vacuuming, dusting, mopping, and cleaning toilets, my mind would wander. There were times I felt so sorry for myself that I wanted to cry. Just weeks before I had been on that stage in Boston, feeding off the energy of the crowd, believing my dream was coming true. And now here I was, feeling worthless and ashamed as I scrubbed rich men's latrines.

4

A Long, Long Way from Home

T
he summer before Black Sheep's demise, I attended a
Spooky Tooth concert at Rochester's Auditorium Theater.
Our connections with Capitol Records enabled us to get
backstage passes, and we met the group after the show. A few
months earlier, the group had lost its lead guitar player, Luther
Grosvenor, and replaced him with an Englishman named Mick
Jones. Our manager gave me a copy of Spooky Tooth's latest
album, and I had noticed that Jones, along with Gary Wright,
was credited with writing the lion's share of the songs. It was
customary for upstart bands like ours to pitch our wares to
established groups, so I gave Mick copies of our two albums.
He didn't seem overwhelmed by my gesture, but I didn't think
anything of it because I'm sure he and his bandmates received
albums from groups trying to break through at virtually every
tour stop. I just figured Mick would toss the vinyls into the trash
before even giving them a listen. Fortunately, that wasn't the case.

The spring after I gave him the albums—the spring of 1976—I was as depressed as hell, feeling as if I were walking around with a sign reading, "World's Biggest Failure." I was barely scraping by—still cleaning those judge's chambers for my public assistance check and picking up additional odd jobs such as refurbishing damaged desks and cabinets and delivering parts from a local car dealership to collision shops. One day during this dark time, my dad told me that he had received a call from some guy in New York City with an English accent who said he had met me during a concert stop in Rochester last summer. "Some guy by the name of Mick Jones," Dad related. My interest was piqued, so I rang Mick up. He told me that he was no longer with Spooky Tooth, the band had broken up, and he was in the process of forming his own band. He said he had listened to the Black Sheep albums and said bluntly that he didn't think much of the band, but he really liked the way I sang and was wondering if I would come to New York for an audition. I thanked him for the offer but told him that Black Sheep is my band and has been my band for five years. I said we were very close to breaking through and that I wasn't the kind of guy who abandons something I start. I ended by saying, "Thanks but no thanks," and wished him well. He said, "Bloke, I understand. But I want you to take some time and give it more serious thought, and I'll call you back in a few weeks."

About a week after that phone call, Black Sheep got together for our recording sessions that were really more like therapy sessions. We didn't do any playing, just talking. During our commiserations, I told the guys about the conversation I had with Mick and how I told him thanks but no thanks because I still had a band. Each of them gazed at me as if I was crazy. I forget who it was, but one of them piped up and said in no

uncertain terms, "You have to go for that audition. You have to."
"Yeah," chimed in another. "What do you have to lose? Lou,
the reality is that we're bottom up here. There is *no* chance of
anything happening for us again. None! You've got to take this
opportunity. And if it works out, at least we can say that one
of us made it."

I know they were looking out for my best interests, but part
of me was upset that they were giving me their blessing because
it gave finality to Black Sheep and I don't think I was ready for
that. I was still grieving, still in denial, and still holding out a
glimmer of hope that we could find a way to revive things and
get another shot. We had poured so much of ourselves into that
band, and I loved the music we had made and our camaraderie
and the fact that we were all small-town guys. I walked out of
that session with a sick feeling in the pit of my stomach. But the
more I thought about it, the more I realized they were right.
Mick, as he said he would, called me back and I told him that
I had rethought things and would like to take him up on his
offer. He sent me a plane ticket, hotel reservations, and some
food and cab money. With conflicted emotions, I flew to New
York. To be honest with you, I didn't think I had a chance in
the world of succeeding at the audition. I fully expected to be
back in Rochester within a day, working at the furniture store
and cleaning those judge's chambers.

I met Mick at his Manhattan recording studio in April
1976. He thanked me for coming down and introduced me to
guitarist Ian McDonald and keyboardist Al Greenwood. The
three of them had already compiled some demos. Mick handed
me a sheet with the lyrics and played the demos that featured
only music, no words. After that, Mick sang the melody for
me into my headphones so that I would know roughly how he

wanted me to sing the song. He then told me to go over to the microphone with the music stand. He rewound the music tape to the beginning and told me to give it a shot. I was so nervous I could feel my knees knocking.

There were three songs they had me do—"Feels Like the First Time," "World at War," and "Take Me to Your Leader." The first two wound up making the cut of Foreigner's first album. Mick had already auditioned about 50 singers, none to his liking, but there was something about my voice on those Black Sheep albums that had caused him to think, *This is the voice I want to carry out the band's vision.* And I guess my audition only confirmed those beliefs, although it took a while for him and the others to convey that to me.

After a few hours of auditioning, they took me to dinner and we talked for a few hours, in order to get to know one another. I told them about my situation in Rochester, but I didn't get into the gory details about me having been on welfare. I was too ashamed to talk about that. But I did want them to know more about my musical background, the bands I had played in and my progression from drummer to vocalist.

At the end of the night, I thanked Mick for the opportunity and asked him what time my flight was the next morning. He said, "Well, we were hoping you could stay another day and rehearse a little bit more and hear you in more live situations." What you have to understand is that neither he nor Ian nor Al had even indicated to me that they liked my voice. I told him I would, so we spent the next day in the recording studio, working on those three songs along with some new tunes. Following that session, we grabbed a bite to eat and I told Mick that I was one of the main writers for my band and it was something I truly loved. I could see him perk up when I told him that, and he asked if

I would stop by his apartment the next day and work on some ideas they had. I agreed, and after that third day, I again thanked him and told him I was heading back to Rochester the next day. He asked me if I could stay another day. I told him I could but that there was just one problem: I only packed for one day, so I was rotating dirty underwear and socks and I'm at the point, from a laundry perspective, that I might become offensive." He laughed and said we could take care of that problem.

The next day I met the band's manager, Bud Prager, for the first time, and we played and talked some more. At the end of that session I told all of them that this had been fun, "But I've already stayed three days longer than I planned, and I have to get back to Rochester and on with my life. Honestly, I don't know if you guys like the way I sing or not. Just tell me if I'm in or out, and we'll go from there." Each of them broke into a smile and looked at me as if I were daft. "You're in, bloke," Mick said in his English accent, patting me on the back. "You're in." Al Greenwood said, "We knew you were the one after the first two lines you sang the first day you were here." I began pumping their hands. To this day, I still don't know the names of any of the guys I had beaten out. I just know that Mick & Co. had gone through a lot of people, and I was the final audition. It's funny, but half of me was ecstatic that I had landed the job of lead vocalist for this new and still-nameless band, but the other half of me was feeling a little blue. In my heart, I guess that faint flicker of a candle still burned for Black Sheep. It was like I was hoping they wouldn't like me so that I could go back and try to revive my band.

When I returned to Rochester and told the guys from Black Sheep that I had landed a spot in the band, they were thrilled, but I was still conflicted. I even told them I was not sure it was what I wanted to do. But they reiterated what a great opportunity it was and that I needed to get over Black Sheep because Black Sheep was dead. My parents could sense my reservations, too, but as difficult as it was for them to see me go, they told me I had to give this my best shot and hope it took off.

Reluctantly, my girlfriend, who would become my first wife, packed what few belongings we had and we headed down the Thruway to New York City. Prager was footing the bill for the band's launching, so I was guaranteed a steady income. With the help of our new drummer, Dennis Elliott, and his wife, we found a tiny apartment for about $150 a month in Ossining near the prison in northern Westchester County, about an hour's drive north from the Manhattan studios we'd be recording in. Although I realized this band had great potential—I really believed that the songs I sang for them while auditioning were going to be hits—I kept my optimism in check. The precipitous demise of Black Sheep and the near-misses of my previous bands made me gun-shy. Despite the impressive backgrounds of some of the musicians in this new band and the initial monetary backing, there were no guarantees this venture would fly. The music business is a real crap shoot. The odds were definitely stacked against us.

The original Foreigner was a sextet with three Brits and three Americans. And that's how we came up with the group's name. Because we had a mix, we said that no matter where we played, in the States or Canada or abroad, there would always be someone performing on foreign soil. We didn't actually come up with the name until after we landed our first contract with Atlantic Records in the summer of 1976. We had been so busy recording songs and preparing our first album that we hadn't given the name much thought. Mick originally suggested the name Trigger, as in the trigger of a gun. He envisioned a drawing of a big gun across our bass drum on stage. When he brought up his suggestion one day, one of the guys made a sound like a horse, because the name reminded him of Roy Rogers' horse, Trigger, in the old western television series. We all started laughing. But Mick wanted to give it a chance, so we did for a real brief time then dropped it for good after we learned that some band already had that name. Mick then suggested Foreigner, and there was a consensus the instant he mentioned it.

Mick was the driving force behind the band's formation and, along with Ian McDonald, was responsible for the recruitment of the other four members, including me. I was clearly the novice of the group and hadn't experienced anywhere near the magnitude of success that Mick and Ian had. I had only become aware of Mick's guitar and songwriting skills after he joined Spooky Tooth. Before joining them, he had worked on backup groups for French pop idols Sylvie Vartan and her husband, Johnny Hallyday, who was known as the French Elvis. Hallyday had the same hair style, the same hip-gyrating onstage moves, and nearly as strong a following in Europe as the King had in the states. Mick was his guitar player, co-writer, and arranger for nearly 10 years and was compensated very well and living high on the hog. So even before he joined Spooky Tooth, he was a well-known personality and musician in Europe.

One of Mick's big claims to fame and best music memories occurred before he hooked up with the French Elvis. As a 19-year-old, Mick played for a French group that opened for the Beatles in Paris in January 1964. George Harrison supposedly took a liking to Mick and would ask him to hop in their limo after shows and go party with them. Later, Mick joined pre-Led Zeppelin members Jimmy Page and John Paul Jones for session work on Hallyday's recordings. After forming a band called Wonderwheel, Mick and keyboardist Gary Wright (who had recorded the hit songs "Dream Weaver" and "Love Is Alive") reformed Spooky Tooth. They recorded three albums in the early 1970s before disbanding. Mick then teamed with Ian McDonald to be backup musicians for Ian Lloyd's solo album in 1976. It was while they were playing together with Lloyd that Mick and McDonald began toying with the idea of forming their own band.

I had been more familiar with Ian's musical background than Mick's. He had performed with King Crimson and before that had enjoyed great success with his McDonald and Giles album in 1971. Ian was an incredibly versatile performer who could play the guitar, keyboards, saxophone, and flute, as well as back up on vocals. Elliott, as I mentioned, was our drummer and also provided back-up vocals. Al Greenwood handled our keyboards and was very good with synthesizers. Ed Gagliardi, a young guy from Long Island, played bass guitar. He was the last to join the group. And I became our lead vocalist and co-songwriter.

To my surprise and delight, we all clicked immediately. I thought when we started rehearsing that there would be a get-to-know-you period where we would be feeling one another out, but it wasn't like that at all. The chemistry among us was instant. We went at it pretty hard right from the start, rehearsing a solid eight hours a day, usually from noon until about 8:00 PM at our Manhattan studios. After the sessions ended, I would head to Mick's apartment where we'd grab some dinner and write until midnight. Then I'd drive back to my apartment in Westchester. They were long days, but I didn't mind at all because I was young and energetic and doing something I had always dreamed of doing.

There was great chemistry between Mick and me during that embryonic period of Foreigner. We were in synch on the same page, and it showed in the music we created. The creative juices flowed freely, and within a matter of a just a few weeks, we had cranked out four songs of fairly high quality. I was feeling great about the songwriting end of it because, to be honest, I didn't really know how much say I would have in that process. What I discovered was that although Mick said he hadn't liked Black Sheep's albums, I discovered that he had liked my voice as well as the lyrics to some of our songs. We had a great exchange of ideas early on, and it was a gas seeing the songs come together with relative ease in an amazingly short period of time.

Mick and Ian had written three or four songs before the rest of us had even joined the band, and those, along with four more that Mick and I collaborated on, gave us a solid demo album that we started pitching to the record companies. The demo wound up garnering serious interest, and we auditioned for each of the major record labels in New York. It was strange because you were performing in a studio in front of a handful of big wigs from a particular record company, so you weren't getting the two-way flow of energy you experience when you perform at a concert. The hope was that the execs would get a feel for your music, your lyrics, your look, and your presentation. Although we felt we had done well and what we offered had great potential, each of the labels turned us down.

Among those rejecting us was Atlantic Records, but their head of A&R (artists and repertoire), John Kalodner, apparently saw something in us that the company's president hadn't. Afterward, he met with us and said that while he could see why we had been rejected, he believed we had a lot of promise. He said that because Mick and I had only started writing together a short while ago, we hadn't yet begun to tap our potential. John suggested we find a good producer and tweak the three songs we had played, and that's what we did. We changed some of the lyrics and melodies and edited the songs down to about three minutes so they would be more radio friendly. Once we became comfortable with the revisions, we invited John back and he was thrilled with what he heard. He then went back to his bosses at Atlantic and convinced them to give us another audition. This time they liked what they heard and signed us to a contract in the early fall of 1976. John was a really cool guy—he often wore white suits, had very long hair and a very long beard, and wore round John Lennon–style glasses. He knew how to open up doors and wound up becoming one of the hottest A&R guys in the music business, achieving success with us and groups like AC/DC.

I also give Bud Prager, our manager, a great deal of credit for helping us land that contract. Bud was very well-respected in the music industry and had a lot of clout. He had achieved success with several bands, including Mountain, which gained fame for its hard-rocking hit, "Mississippi Queen," and for playing at Woodstock. We were very fortunate to have Bud manage us for 17 years. A lot of bands never make it because they are mismanaged. He was constantly hustling on our behalf, working the phones, and his pitching resulted in John giving us that second look. Heck, Bud believed so deeply in us that he cashed in part of a pension package he had to fund us until we got our break. He put his money where his mouth was and, fortunately, we were able to reward his faith in us.

I was thrilled with the news of our deal with Atlantic because they were one of the heavy hitters in the music business. They were the label for artists such as the Stones, Aretha Franklin, and

Led Zeppelin. When you walked into their recording studios, you could feel the history in the air. This was huge. Still, I didn't allow myself to become too giddy. The fate that befell Black Sheep remained painfully vivid. That kept me grounded, kept me from doing cartwheels. And the rest of my bandmates seemed to be cautiously optimistic, too. We all realized this was merely a first step, albeit a very big one, and that there was much work to be done before we could truly celebrate. The game plan was for us to have the album ready by the following March and begin touring to promote it that spring and summer. Our goal was to have 10 songs on the album, which meant we needed to write and record about 14 songs to choose from.

As I said, everybody appeared to be in synch from the get-go. Mick was a superb lead guitarist—his riffs were sharp all the time and provided the solid foundation for our early songs. You could hang your lyrics on his notes. Greenwood was an exceptional keyboard player. Ian's brilliance and versatility was evident regardless if we needed him to play the guitar, keyboards, sax, or flute. Elliott was a fabulous drummer who had once played for the British group IF, which was the English version of Blood, Sweat and Tears. There had been some concern that since his background had been more with jazz rock that he might be a little light with his drumming, but he wasn't. He provided the heavy-handed playing we needed for our hard-rock style. Dennis was a really interesting guy away from the music scene. He was a very skilled woodworker. In fact, he was so passionate about it that he would leave Foreigner and the music industry in 1992 to pursue woodworking full-time.

I think everybody, with the exception of bass guitarist Gagliardi, discovered their roles fairly easily. Ed was the least experienced and accomplished member—his background was mostly with cover bands—and he and Mick locked horns from the beginning of our rehearsals. Mick wanted the bass sound to be simple, and Ed had a tendency to overplay things. There were many times when Mick would stop the song and have to demonstrate to Ed what he wanted. Ed could be a little stubborn at times, but eventually he would acquiesce, finally realizing that Mick was vastly more accomplished and had a better idea of what made songs work than he did.

The recording process can be both rewarding and aggravating. It's a tedious endeavor to be sure. We'd spend days, sometimes weeks, fine-tuning songs. After a session, I often would take a demo cassette tape and play it in my car on the way home. And I'd pop it back in the next morning on my return trip to the studio. Other members would do the same, and then we'd each offer our input. At times, these sessions could become quite heated, and somebody would stomp out and not come back until the next day. During these stressful times, the disparate personalities of our members were revealed. Mick had quite a temper, as did Dennis, and when they butted heads, which was often, you were fearful they were going to come to blows. But that tension was understandable considering we had six guys spending 12–14 hours a day with one another often cooped up in a studio. You were with each other much more than you were with your significant other, and the familiarity occasionally bred contempt.

Early on, everybody was so passionate about creating the best sound possible—and that was a good thing. Later on, after we had achieved big-time success, egos became inflated and got in the way of things. The creative exchanges ceased to exist, and that led to the band's demise. But more on that later.

It occasionally took months before we came to a consensus about a song. In some cases, we did so much tweaking that by the time we finished a song, it bore little resemblance to what we had started with. And more times than not, you tweaked and tweaked and tweaked some more before reaching the conclusion that this song was going nowhere and you needed to move on to something else.

After working non-stop for several months, we completed the songs for our album, and we were quite pleased with the finished product. I felt good that we had several potential hits on our hands, but I tempered my optimism. There was still that feeling in the pit of my stomach that this could turn out like it did for Black Sheep. And I realized I probably wasn't going to be able to shake that feeling until we had produced several successful albums.

The music industry was an entirely different animal back then. The Internet didn't exist. You couldn't download songs onto your computer or MP3 player or iPod or smart phone. Radio had enormous listenership, and it could make or break you. You had to get as much airplay as you could and hope people responded by calling in to request your songs and, of course, by buying your records and albums and concert tickets. Shortly after New Year's Day 1977, Atlantic decided to release the single, "Feels Like the First Time," from our first album, which was titled Foreigner. (Naming your first album after your band was a common practice back then.)

I thought the choice of "First Time" was a wise strategy because the record had a hard-driving sound with memorable lyrics and I believed it would take off, which it did. The approach in the 1960s and 1970s was to flood as many radio stations as you could with your record in hopes that at least a third to a half of them would play it regularly. But Atlantic decided to take a more targeted approach with us. Rather than shotgun it to every station and hope for the best, Atlantic decided to initially release it only to the most popular rock stations in the biggest markets, stations such as WNEW-FM in New York and KLOS in Los Angeles. The rationale was that after we drummed up interest with the power stations, the other stations in those big markets as well as the mid-sized market stations would be clamoring to get their hands on the record, too.

When I said radio could make or break you, I meant specifically disc jockeys could make or break you. And back then every city had powerful ones—people like Scott Muni in New York City and Kid Leo in Cleveland. Muni was known as "The Professor" because of his encyclopedic knowledge of rock 'n' roll. All the big names from Lennon to Jagger to Springsteen would stop by his studio to do live interviews and pitch their latest songs. There's a funny story about how Led Zeppelin guitarist Jimmy Page was being interviewed by Muni one time and collapsed to the floor in mid-sentence, apparently wiped out by several days of heavy partying. The unflappable Professor simply put on a Zeppelin record, revived Page, and resumed the interview after the song ended as if nothing had happened. If guys like Muni or Kid Leo chatted you up and played your stuff, it could mean thousands of additional record and concert sales. And if they trashed you, it could really undermine your single or album's chances for success. So you really had to do everything in your power to kiss their asses and make them like you so they would play your stuff. These guys definitely were well aware of the game being played and of the power they wielded. Many of these DJs had egos as big as a rock star's. Some of them would really make you jump through hoops and bust your chops during interviews before finally playing your song. It wasn't always a pleasant process—in fact, at times it felt kind of slimy—but you had to take part in order to survive and hopefully flourish.

We were fortunate because our manager, Bud Prager, knew how to promote things and massage the DJs to get us on their shows. Bud was a master at it. He knew all the ins and outs of the music business, and he worked his butt off on our behalf.

Interestingly, it was Bud who was responsible for me shortening my stage name to Gramm. Before our first album was finished, he took me into his office for a chat. "Lou, I don't want to offend you—this is just a suggestion—but I think you should shorten your name, make it less ethnic-sounding, make it easier to pronounce," he said. "Even though people have become more accepting, there's still some bias against people with immigrant names. I don't agree with it. It's just the way it is. Plus, we're going to have you do a lot of interviews on radio and television and in print, and we don't want people to start butchering and misspelling and mispronouncing your name. Again, this is only a suggestion. And if you don't want to do it, I understand completely." I sat there stunned. Growing up in Rochester, a true melting pot, I encountered people daily with Italian, German, Polish, Jewish, and Irish surnames. I never gave it a second thought. But I understood what Bud was saying. Although we had come a long way, people were still discriminated against based on their ethnicity. After giving it some thought, I agreed, but I told him it was only a stage name, that my legal name would remain Grammatico, and he was fine with that. The tough part was breaking the news to my parents. I tried to explain it to them the way Bud had to me, telling them that I loved my name and that, legally, it would always be Grammatico. But they were quite upset, and I understood why. "What?" my father said indignantly. "Aren't you proud of your heritage?" I told him it had nothing to do with that, but he was very upset. And it took a while for him to accept that it was only a stage name, that I still was and would always be Lou Grammatico. When we finally did achieve success and people requested my autograph, it took me a while to get used to signing the shortened version of my name.

We were coming onto the scene at a time when disco was starting to fade and punk rock was all the rage. I didn't care much for disco, but I did like some punk rock, especially groups like The Clash. There was clearly a void as far as rock 'n' roll groups were concerned, so our timing was good. Bruce Springsteen, Fleetwood Mac, and the Eagles had exploded onto the scene, and our trail had been blazed by the likes of contemporaries such as Boston, The Cars, and Cheap Trick. Boston and its self-titled debut album became a landmark record and really opened the door for us and several other groups hoping to make a name for themselves while reviving rock 'n' roll. As I said, we were really pleased with the album we had put together. We were fortunate not only to have some really gifted musicians in the band but to have some musicians who played with personality. And that really showed in that first album. You could turn your attention to any instrument in any of those songs and hear that the artist was really into what he was doing.

Atlantic Records went all out in promoting us and our new album. They took out a full-page ad in *Rolling Stone* magazine. It featured a huge photo of us and the album cover with the headline: "It's Not Where They Came From…It's Where They're Going." The ad copy mentioned that Foreigner's members had come from some respected bands.

"And today, Mick Jones, Ian McDonald, Lou Gramm, Al Greenwood, Ed Gagliardi, and Dennis Elliott bring all that musical savvy and experience to their new group, with some of the most dynamic rock 'n' roll you've ever heard.

"Foreigner. They're not going to be strangers for long."

Our confidence was immediately boosted when "Feels Like the First Time" shot up the charts, peaking at No. 4 midway through 1977. Interestingly, that was the first song Mick had me sing when I came down to audition for the band. Although it was already written by the time I joined Foreigner, I had some input in the final product. I helped change some of the lyrics because the way Mick wrote it was how an Englishman rather than an American would sing it. I remember improvising the way an actor might with his lines during our rehearsals, and he would stop me and say, "No, no, no, it's supposed to be such-and-such," and I would say, "I don't speak like that." We'd go back and forth a bit, and finally he relented and allowed me to Americanize it. We'd have similar exchanges like that on many other songs we collaborated on. Sometimes he would say, "That's cool," and sometimes he would insist that I sing it the way he wrote it.

Like I said, Mick and I had a good working relationship on those early albums. We were fortunate in that we wrote in a very similar fashion. He would provide me a cassette with some guitar riffs he had been working on, and I would work on a lyric and melody that were compatible. Then we would put the words and the music together and fine-tune it, and a song would develop from that collaboration.

The first song we actually worked on together was "Long, Long Way from Home." The title and lyrics were autobiographical. There's a line in the song, "I left a small town for the Apple in decay," an obvious reference to my journey from little old Rochester to the concrete canyons of Manhattan. People forget, but the mid- to late-1970s were tough times for New York. The city was on the brink of bankruptcy. Crime was rampant. I'll never forget when I went there for my Foreigner audition, New York was in the midst of a long strike by the sanitation engineers, and the garbage was stacked several feet high on the sidewalks. It was rancid. And not long after that, the Big Apple was dealing with the Son of Sam serial murders. New Yorkers are known for being tough, weathered, world-wary people, but that string of murders chilled them to the core.

• • •

Mick was a charmer and could be fun to be around, but he also had a tendency to be a taskmaster who could rub people the wrong way. He was clearly at the top of his game in those early years of Foreigner. His creativity and his instincts for music were something to behold. Although I respected his abilities, I didn't believe I was out of my league—not even a little bit—but I knew this was going to be something that was going to challenge me. If I was going to be one of the main writers for the band, I had better rise to the occasion. And I believe I did. My confidence in my ability to write songs grew rapidly. In those formative years, I was bubbling over with ideas. And it seemed that just about everything and anything I broached, Mick liked. Later on, that wouldn't be the case. He became more dismissive and started rejecting just about everything I suggested, which led to the deterioration of our relationship and the band.

That relationship between songwriters is an interesting waltz indeed. You often step on one another's toes and egos along the way. And that's okay if some creative tension exists— in fact, that can lead to some great music. But there has to be respect on both sides in order for it to truly work. There has to be an honest give-and-take, a two-way street. And I think we had that for a while and produced many songs that became rock classics.

I had a good rapport with Ian McDonald. We worked on a couple of songs together—just the two of us—and I believed they were pretty good, but Mick thought otherwise. He liked Ian's musical expertise and his ability to play several different instruments—and play them well—but it was apparent that Mick didn't think too much of Ian's songwriting skills. And that resulted in a wall building up between the two fairly early.

Dennis Elliott and I became good friends. As I mentioned, he and his wife helped me and my first wife find our first apartment in Westchester County, and the four of us enjoyed each other's company immensely. We'd spend a lot of time at each other's places and often go out to restaurants together.

Al Greenwood was a quiet guy and a little difficult to get to know. He wasn't standoffish, he just kind of kept to himself a little more, not as open and outgoing, but he was a great guy. He always wanted to participate in the writing process, too. He would present us with song ideas that we didn't care for that much, but when he worked on someone else's songs, he was truly brilliant. He really was a keyboard genius. He was a very important part of our success.

Like I said, Ed Gagliardi was the least experienced and accomplished musician in the band, and he and Mick had some memorable arguments. It took a while for Ed to accept his role and play the bass the way we needed it to be played. He wasn't a bad guy, he just was a little headstrong and had his own ideas that weren't always compatible with what we were trying to accomplish.

• • •

"Cold as Ice," the second hit from that first album, was a three-way collaboration between Mick, Ian, and me. That was actually one of the few songs where the three of us worked together. The inspiration was from a scene in an old Bette Davis movie in which she played this tough aloof babe. Later, that song would be used in a comedic skit on *Saturday Night Live* in which John Belushi is dressed like a hoodlum in a trenchcoat and fedora and tries to come on to this buxom bombshell. All of a sudden, she pulls a gun out of her purse and shoots him about 30 times as the song keeps playing. We had no advance warning that they were going to use the song, but we were thrilled to tears because SNL was hugely popular and it was a great promotion for the song.

Through the years, our music would appear in a number of television shows, commercials, even movies. Perhaps the most bizarre media play Foreigner received was during a 2002 episode of the *Aqua Teen Hunger Force*, a hip adult-animation weekly series that aired on The Cartoon Network. We can thank our merchandise people for inspiring this particular script. Back in the early 1980s, when we were really flying high, some merchandise whiz came up with the not-so-brilliant idea of adding a glitzy Foreigner belt buckle to our line of souvenir offerings that included T-shirts, baseball caps, etc. The buckles were pretty garish-looking, with plenty of glitter and a humungous "F" in the middle. Two decades later, one of the quirky, creative writers of *Aqua Teen* decided to build a plot around the Foreigner belt buckle, bestowing secret powers upon it. The three main *Aqua Teen* characters were fast-food items with faces and legs and arms. One was an animated milkshake named Master Shake. Another was a talking hamburger (Meatwad), while a third was a french fry (Frylock.) In order to activate the buckle's superpowers, the characters had to shout out the titles of various Foreigner songs. I know this sounds like some acid-inspired episode, but it really did air. And when we saw it, we were laughing so hard we almost wet our pants.

Speaking of french fries, one of the companies that utilized our music was Burger King. They used our song, "Double Vision," as part of their 1997 ad campaign to promote their new $2.22 meal packages which included two hamburgers and two orders of fries. They took some photos of me chomping on a burger, which was kind of funny because by that point, I had cut out fast foods. So much for truth in advertising, but hey, it was a great way for us to get additional airplay on television and the radio.

5

No Foreigner to Success

Our first album was released in March 1977, about four weeks after "Feels Like the First Time" hit the airwaves. By that time, Prager had booked us to tour with the Doobie Brothers, who were one of the hottest acts going. They had just released their *Taking It to the Streets* album with Michael McDonald singing the lead, and they were at the height of their popularity, playing big sheds—14,000-16,000–seat arenas. When I first learned we would be opening for them, I thought it was a strange pairing because our music had a much harder edge, and the Doobie Brothers' fans wouldn't appreciate it. But I was totally wrong. We toured for three or four months, and it worked out great. I think having contrasting bands actually helped. If we were more of a light rock band like the Doobies or the Doobies were hard-edged like us, that might have made for a long evening. It was actually a great strategy to contrast different music styles. The Doobie fans really responded to us. And even though we were just the warm-up band and they were the headliners, the Doobie Brothers were very good to us, very encouraging.

When I look back it's kind of funny because we had a hit record out there before we had played our first concert together. Everything had come together well in the studio, but there's a huge difference between recording sessions, where you do bits and pieces over and over again then splice them together until it sounds perfect, and live concerts, where the conditions aren't so perfect and there's an audience out there with expectations. Before we began our official tour with the Doobie Brothers, Bud arranged for us to play free concerts—one in front of a small audience at The Bayou, a little club in the Georgetown area of Washington, D.C., that had a maximum capacity of about 400 people, and another in front of about 15,000 people at American University. Although we had developed a good chemistry in the studio and had played each of our songs a thousand times, we all were a little nervous about how we'd do in front of a live audience. I remember having big-time butterflies before those debut shows. And I remember moving around the stage like a crazy man because I had so much nervous energy. I had to tell myself to chill a little or I was going to be gassed by about the third or fourth song. Fortunately, the concerts were rousing successes. The audiences really responded to us, and I think part of that was due to the fact that "Feels Like the First Time" and several of our other album cuts received extensive airplay. So when we took the stage, people were already familiar with our songs to the point that they were singing the lyrics right along with us.

I mentioned how radio promotion and air play were essential to a band's success. Well, tours were huge, too. That was how you pushed record sales and created an even greater buzz for your albums and your band. You'd usually wait until about a month to six weeks after your album was released to hit the road. That way it had received quite a bit of air play, and people were familiar with your latest songs. We hit the road just as "Feels Like the First Time" was flying up the charts and just as AOR (album oriented rock) stations—mostly on the FM band—had begun playing the cuts from our album that you wouldn't normally hear on the Top 40 AM stations. That created familiarity with our music and grew our audience, so when we started touring, people were rocking right along with us.

I was all excited when we first started touring because this was something I dreamed about ever since reading about the Beatles hitting the road. What I didn't know at the time is that the Beatles went on tour for just a few weeks. We were going to be nomads for nearly four months, but at least we'd be carted around in our luxury bus. And that was a huge upgrade from my Black Sheep days when Jim Taylor's huge Ford Galaxie was our mode of transportation.

It didn't take long to learn how rigorous touring can be. The glamour disappears quickly. The touring company gave us a bus that was already about a dozen years old with more than 500,000 miles on the odometer. Its engine had been rebuilt two or three times. On occasion the air conditioning didn't work and the latrine would back up. The Doobies, meanwhile, had a brand-new bus that was bigger and featured many more amenities. It was a reminder that we were still upstarts. I'll never forget the leg between Phoenix and Los Angeles. It was toward the end of the tour, when most of us were spent and couldn't wait for some time away, and our bus broke down in the middle of Death Valley. The bus immediately became like a hot box. We opened the windows, but that just made it worse because it was more than 100 degrees outside and that desert sun was baking us like a turkey in an oven. These were the days long before cell phones. There weren't any signs of civilization for as far as the eye could see. In the evening, when the sun began to set and it started to cool down a tad, the driver was able to fix the radiator leak and get the rig moving again. We pulled into L.A. about six hours late, feeling like burnt toast.

One of our funnier tour experiences occurred many years later when we pulled off the highway to gas up the bus and grab some munchies at a 7-Eleven with a service station attached to it. We had just played a show in West Virginia, and I believe our next show was in Michigan. It was about four in the morning, and while the driver was filling up the tank, everybody got off the bus, except Mick, who was asleep in his bunk. We got our snacks and got back on the bus and Mick's brother, Kevin, who was our tour manager, did a head count and figured Mick was still sleeping in his bunk because the curtain was drawn shut. We motored out of the lot and onto the highway and traveled for about three or four hours and were just about to reach our destination when Kevin goes to wake up Mick and discovers that there's nobody there. Unbeknownst to us, Mick had gotten off the bus at the 7-Eleven, too. After we re-boarded, we took off, figuring he was still asleep in his bunk. Mick didn't have his cell with him and didn't have our numbers, so he wound up calling his mother in England, who finally got a hold of Kevin. "You left your brother back at the 7-Eleven," she told him. So we turned the bus around and headed back to pick him up. That added an extra seven or eight hours to our trip, and we wound up getting to our next concert with little time to spare. We didn't even have time to check in to our hotel—we had to go straight to the arena.

During that first tour, we'd play an average of four to five nights a week, anywhere from 45 minutes to an hour each show.

Then we'd get cleaned up and watch the Doobies play, and after they were done, we'd head back to the hotel and make a beeline to the bar. You were still riding an adrenaline high from the concert; you were too revved up to sleep. So you'd blow off steam either in the bar or in one of the suites. There were many nights that ended with me seeing the sun rise, and then it would be time to get back on the bus and head for the next stop as we dealt with severe hangovers and fatigue. We had televisions and VCRs on the bus, so you'd spend plenty of time watching movies. We'd also play a lot of cards—never for money, just to while away the endless hours on the road.

They would build in a couple days of breaks during the tours when you could actually return home to your family. But it was really tough because you wouldn't be home long enough to really decompress and get into any kind of normal routine with your wife and kids. They'd be winding down at 10:00 or 11:00 at night just as you were used to revving up. It was a screwed-up situation and very difficult to deal with.

The frequency of our concerts and the length of our tours occasionally would take a toll on my vocal cords. Performing four to five shows a week was brutal on my pipes. We were a loud, loud band, so I'd have to really belt out our songs to be heard over our guitars and drums and keyboards. And then I'd be called upon to hit the high notes on our rock ballads. After the third night in a row, my voice would be shot. As we became more successful, I pleaded with management to change the sequence of the concert schedule. I suggested no more than three nights in a row. I thought we'd be better off if we were three nights on, two nights off, two nights on, one night off. But they never listened to me, and we'd reach certain points of the tour where my voice would start to go. I'd attempt to sing a certain note and nothing but air would come out. I'd have to grind my way through the rest of the song and concert, even singing around some of the high notes. The next day I'd have to go to a throat specialist. He'd look at my throat with his flashlight and say, "Lou, you've got to shut it down for 10 days because your vocal cords look like chopped liver." And our tour manager would be ready to faint because that meant we would have to postpone shows. We'd wind up compromising, and I'd take off three or four days then go right back at it.

As my career progressed, I learned some tricks of the trade to keep my voice in peak condition despite the abuse of overuse. I wouldn't talk during the day, I cut out carbonated drinks, and I stuck to room-temperature water. Several minutes before we took the stage, I would start doing the scales to loosen up my cords, kind of like an athlete doing pre-game stretching. And we would build in longer-than-usual guitar and drum solos to give me a chance to rest my instrument. Between our first and second tours, our manager suggested I work with a voice coach he knew who had worked with many Broadway stars, including singer Liza Minnelli and Tony Award–winning actor Joel Gray. The thinking was that Amri Galli-Campi would help me learn some breathing techniques and vocal exercises that would help me better withstand the rigors of our stacked concert schedules. I thought it was a good idea and wound up taking lessons from Campi, a former star soprano with the Metropolitan Opera who lived in this Manhattan apartment so tiny you had to turn sideways to make it through the hallway. She taught me how to warm up with scales, how to do breathing exercises to open up the diaphragm to get the most air out, and how to sing the entire line of a verse before needing to take a breath. I got a kick out of going there because she had no idea who I was or what kind of music I sang. I remember early on practicing my scales in her study and Campi said, "Boy oh boy, how are you ever going to make it with a voice like that?" I started laughing. She was so cute. But she knew her stuff. The lessons I learned wound up being very helpful. Still are.

My attire with Foreigner wasn't much different from my attire from my garage band days with Black Sheep. And it would remain that way throughout most of my career. While the Brits in the band wore dress shirts with sports coats or vests and designer jeans with perfect creases—which I thought was kind of squirrelly—I stuck with my sleeveless T-shirts, un-creased jeans, and sneakers. I was a rocker, not a model. I wanted to be comfortable on stage. With me, it was always about the music, not fashion. Of course, I might have been reluctant to wear what I did if I hadn't gotten myself into very good shape. Early on, we began touring with a fitness trainer, who made us work out virtually every day we were on the road, which was a good thing because touring was grueling. He'd scope out gyms in various cities where we could train, and he kept on us. Even if we hadn't gotten to bed until 2:00 in the morning, he'd have us up at 7:00, pumping iron or running on a treadmill some place. I'm glad he did because bouncing around the stage for two or three hours can take its toll.

• • •

Spurred by great radio play and our tour, our first album became an enormous success, yielding three hits and selling five million copies—including a phenomenal one million records in the first month after its release. It spent 113 weeks—more than two years!—on *Billboard*'s best-selling album chart, and the magazine named us top new artist of the year. We were even nominated for a Grammy. But despite the accolades, I knew we hadn't arrived by any means. Rock 'n' roll lore was littered with stories about one-album wonders. We still had a long way to go to avoid that painful label of being a fluke.

• • •

One of my big thrills occurred after the tour when I received my first royalty check. I don't remember the exact amount, but it was close to six figures—more money than I knew existed. We were in dire need of a new car and some things around the house, so that's where some of the money went. After our second album, I bought a modest house in Westchester County. I could have lived in the city, but the Rochester guy in me longed for a yard to mow and neighborhoods and places where our dog could roam. We purchased a 1,500-sq.-ft. house with about 2¼ acres of land, and I became a full-fledged suburbanite who would listen to broadcasts of my Mets getting crushed while mowing my lawn.

As a songwriter, you're always in search of that memorable phrase and theme that will resonate with listeners—words that prompt people to sing the songs out loud. You never know where you might find the inspiration you need, which is why I always carried a notebook with me. I was constantly filling those books with phrases and observations that might work their way into a song. They might come from something I heard on the nightly news or in a movie or something I had read in a novel or from a conversation I overheard in the checkout line at my local grocery store.

In the case of "Double Vision," my inspiration came from a hockey game.

A little background information is in order.

I had been a hockey fan since attending Rochester Americans minor league games at the War Memorial when I was a kid. After we had some success with our first album and I finally had a little extra cash in my pocket, I purchased season tickets to New York Rangers games in Madison Square Garden. One night I couldn't go because we were in our recording studio, but I had a tiny television propped up with duct tape in my vocal booth and I put on the game while Mick was working with some of the guys on this really cool guitar riff. We had been at this particular song for weeks and we all believed it had the potential to be a classic rocker, but there was just one problem—we hadn't been able to find a catchy title and the lyrics to match the music—and that was so frustrating.

That night, while gazing at my miniature TV during my break from rehearsing, I found my inspiration from Rangers hockey goalie John Davidson. The Rangers were playing the Buffalo Sabres in the Stanley Cup playoffs, and during a flurry in front of the net, one of the Sabres elbowed Davidson in the head. He was knocked woozy and had to be helped to the locker room to be examined by the team doctor. I was watching intently when, a few minutes later, one of the announcers came on with an update about Davidson's condition. He said the goalie was going to be all right, but that he had been experiencing some double vision. Voila! A siren went off in my head. Double vision. Perfect.

I shut off the TV and began writing down some lyrics. The instant I started singing them, I knew I was on to something. After working on them for a bit, I bolted excitedly from my booth and told Mick and the guys that I had solved our problem. They looked at me like I was crazy at first, but after I told them about double vision and began singing some of the lyrics, they were excited, too—so excited that we wound up making it the title track of our second album. And that's how it sometimes happens in the wacky world of songwriting. You suffer from writer's block for days, weeks, even months, and then seemingly out of nowhere, it comes to you. I had always been inquisitive and enjoyed observing people in different settings and situations. And that's why I carried those pads around with me. You just never knew where your next song might come from.

When Rangers officials found out that I was really into hockey, they asked me to sing the National Anthem before one of their playoff games at the Garden. The Rangers wound up winning the game and asked me back to sing it again because they thought maybe I could be a good luck charm, like Kate Smith had been for the Flyers with her booming rendition of "God Bless America." Unfortunately, because of scheduling conflicts, I wasn't able to do it. Several years later, Davidson called to see if I would serve as an honorary coach for the Rangers old-timers game. Faster than you could say "Double Vision," I said yes. That was a really cool experience because I got to meet all these guys I had enjoyed watching—players such as Phil Esposito, Ron Dugay, and Dave and Don Maloney. But the biggest thrill was meeting Davidson. When I told him the story about how he was the inspiration for "Double Vision," he thought I was pulling his leg. I recounted what the announcers had said while he was being helped off the ice. I said, "John, I was screaming so loud when that idea came to me that I'm surprised you didn't hear me from our Manhattan studio." He joked that I owed him royalties. We had a good laugh and have talked on occasion through the years.

• • •

We released the *Double Vision* album in June 1978 and started promoting it with the single, "Hot Blooded," which immediately shot up the charts, peaking at No. 3 on the Billboard charts and becoming our first million-selling single. One critic said that "Hot Blooded" was this generation's version of the Stones' "Honky Tonk Woman" and Free's "All Right Now," two catchy rockers that became instant classics. Given my love of those two bands and those two songs, that compliment meant the world to me.

We employed the same marketing strategy we had the first time around, giving the super DJs in the major markets first crack at it before hitting the secondary and tertiary markets. We could tell it was different this time around when we began hitting the road for our series of promotional interviews. The success of our self-titled first album had definitely opened doors for us, and this time the DJs were contacting us for interviews. But there was still skepticism about us, and we got a lot of questions about whether we were worried that our second album might suck. Although we were extremely pleased with the songs we wrote and recorded the second time around, in the back of our minds we were worried, too. Only time and listeners and record-buyers and concert-goers would tell.

We actually debuted an unfinished version of "Hot Blooded" after the end of our first concert tour in March 1978. In those days, they staged this morning-to-midnight mega-concert in California. It was called Cal-Jam and, like Woodstock, it featured at least a dozen different bands. The big groups of the day— the Eagles, Fleetwood Mac, Bob Seger—would play in the evening, and they would invite up-and-coming bands to play in the morning and afternoon. Bill Graham, who was a big West Coast rock promoter, apparently liked what he heard and invited us to play. He told us that we would be at the bottom of the totem pole, meaning we would open the concert at 8:00 AM, but we didn't care because we realized this was a huge, huge break and we would be part of something special.

I vividly remember Bill taking Mick and I up onto the stage about an hour before we were going to play. "I want you to see something really cool," he said. We looked out from the stage and saw the sun just beginning to peek over the mountains. The vista was absolutely breathtaking, and it may still be the most remarkable setting I've ever seen for a concert. "Now, watch what's going to happen," Bill said. Way off in the distance, the guards began to open the gates and you could see this sea of people gush into this massive open field in front of us. Before you knew it, that field was filled with several hundred thousand people. I'll never forget that scene for as long as I live.

As we were about to take our places to kick off the concert, Bill shook our hands and told us to "knock 'em dead, boys." Our job was to set the tone for the day and, to be honest with you, I didn't know how it would go because it was still relatively early in the morning and we had never done a breakfast concert before. But this crowd was into it like it was 8:00 at night instead of 8:00 in the morning. They were ready to rock 'n' roll from that first cup of joe, and so were we. We wound up playing every song from our first album and mixed in a few soulful tunes, such as "Somebody's Been Sleeping in My Bed" by 100 Proof and "Let Me Be Your Love-Maker, Let Me Be Your Soul-Shaker" by Betty Wright.

As we left the stage, the people gave us a thunderous ovation and began chanting, "We want more! We want more!" as we walked off the stage. The roar continued, and backstage Bill walked over to us, beaming, and said, "Go play another song, boys." We looked at one another and said, "Bill, we don't have another song." We instantly realized that we had better come up with one in a hurry because this was an encore opportunity we couldn't refuse. After a few anxious seconds, we decided to go out there and play "Hot Blooded," even though the song was far from finished. I had done a couple of scratch vocals for it, but we had only completed the lyrics for one verse. No big deal. I wound up singing the first verse twice, and then we went into the guitar riffs and dragged the song out a bit. Although the audience had never heard the song before, the people went bonkers. Afterward, when we were in the dressing room, we were slapping each other on the back. It had been an unbelievable gig for us, and their reaction to "Hot Blooded," an unknown single, let us know that we already had one hit ready to launch from our second album.

• • •

Atlantic Records and our manager, Bud Prager, arranged for us to tour with Heart to promote our second album. With lead singers Ann and Nancy Wilson, Heart had made a name for themselves with mega hits such as "Magic Man" and "Crazy on You." They were an established band, but we didn't believe they were worlds ahead of us at this point, the way the Doobie Brothers had been, so it was a good pairing, almost like a 1 and a 1A, instead of a 1 and a 2. The guys in Heart were very friendly, but the women were kind of standoffish, and that was okay with us. We were looking forward to not only pushing our second album but in establishing ourselves as headline material, too. As it turned out, that goal was realized a year sooner than we expected, much to our surprise and Heart's chagrin.

About halfway through the tour, our second album was on fire, with two hits climbing the charts and several of our lesser-known cuts being played regularly on AOR (album oriented radio.) At concerts, the audience began responding more enthusiastically to us than to Heart. The crowds started clamoring for us to go longer than the 45 minutes we were allotted as the opening act.

The concert promoter noticed this, too, and one day he pulled aside Bud and Heart's manager and said he was flip-flopping the acts. When Bud told us that we were going to be the headliner and Heart would open for us, we thought he was pulling our legs. But we finally realized he wasn't joking, and we were ecstatic because this was obviously another indication that we were making a name for ourselves. The members of Heart were shocked, too, and embarrassed and angry. All of a sudden, there was a lot of tension between the two bands, and I understood completely. Had the roles been reversed, I would have been ticked and wouldn't be congenial to the people who had taken my place.

The move was unprecedented, and it immediately put an extra burden on our shoulders. We had to step it up another notch or two so there wouldn't be any doubt about us deserving to be the main act. One of the adjustments we needed to make immediately was expanding our playing time from 45 minutes to roughly two hours. Bud told us that we needed to take advantage of this situation right away because if we struggled, the tour promoter could reverse the roles again.

We didn't waste any time proving we deserved the top spot. The audience feedback was fantastic, and the reviewers proved kind. They liked how we had followed our breakthrough album with one nearly as successful, and they cited the broad spectrum of our music, which included everything from hard rock to ballads. As we got deeper into the tour, the uncertainty I had felt from the Black Sheep fiasco finally began to fade and I began to believe that we weren't flukes, we were a rock band to be reckoned with. That's not to say I was overly cocky. I still knew how fragile this business was and that you had to keep going hard at it and keep creating new music. But I had finally reached a point where I was savoring the success we had achieved and I was looking forward optimistically to even more success.

The bus we rode for our second tour was more modern and spacious with AC that actually worked. Atlantic Records also arranged for us to travel to some places on a special jet they had purchased for our use—a four-engine Viscount with the word *Foreigner* painted in big blue letters on the fuselage. It was another indication that we were, in their eyes, one of their more valued recording groups.

The *Double Vision* album, which, in addition to the title track and "Hot Blooded," featured chart-topper, "Blue Morning, Blue Day," sold five million copies, a million more than our original album. We were definitely on the ascent, and toward the end of our second tour Bud told us that we had been booked for an international tour in Europe and the Far East. Even though we wouldn't be the headliners, it was still very much worth our while because it would expose us to new markets and lay the groundwork that would help us sell millions of records in the coming years.

In the fall of 1978, we made a tour stop in Kansas City that didn't go especially well in Mick's mind. After the concert he really laid into Dennis Elliott, telling him that his drum playing that night had been atrocious. Dennis was furious and went after Mick. He threw his right fist toward Mick's head, but Mick was able to dodge the punch at the last second and Dennis wound up smashing his hand against the door. The blow turned out to be costly—Dennis broke his hand and we had to find a fill-in drummer to finish the tour. The incident had been incited by Mick, who could be quite acerbic at times, and it underscored the smoldering tensions that were building in the band.

The show went on without Dennis—he was replaced by British drummer Ian Wallace who had played with Spooky Tooth, Peter Frampton, and Bob Dylan. The situation made Dennis a little insecure, and as soon as his hand healed enough for him to pick up the sticks, he was back playing, right alongside Ian, so we had a two-drummer thing going for a few months because Dennis' hand wasn't strong enough to make it through an entire concert early on.

The highlight of the tour for me occurred on Saturday night, December 2, 1978, when Foreigner played in my hometown for the first time. I was hoping for a triumphant return, and it wound up being that—and more. The band was riding high at the time of our Rochester appearance—our second album, *Double Vision*, had climbed to No. 5 on the charts and had achieved multiple-platinum status. And unlike most hard-rock bands of that era, we had shown a knack for selling singles as well, with six songs from our first two albums achieving Top 20 recognition, including four that peaked at No. 6 or higher.

In addition to Cal Jam II, our tours had included appearances with the Rolling Stones in front of 100,000 fans at RFK Stadium in Philadelphia and with Fleetwood Mac before 65,000 at Rich Stadium in suburban Buffalo. Playing in Rich was extra cool for me because it was the home of the Buffalo Bills, the football team I had followed passionately for years. (I would later return to the stadium several times to perform the National Anthem during the Bills Super Bowl years in the early 1990s.) That day-long concert at Rich Stadium featured sky divers and a high-wire act by Delilah Wallenda, one of the members of the famous Flying Wallendas. A month before coming to Rochester, we had headlined a sold-out charity concert at Madison Square Garden in the Big Apple.

Although I was exhausted from being on the road for so long—we had done something like 109 or 110 concerts in just more than a year—I couldn't wait to perform in front of my relatives and friends. My hometown was special to me—so special that I would return there permanently in 1988—and I wanted in the worst way to put on a great performance. And I wanted my bandmates to see that Rochester was a big-league city when it came to rock concerts.

A small part of me also wanted to stick it to the club owners and naysayers who had dissed me and Black Sheep. In an advance story in the local newspaper, I told reporter Dave Stearns that the life of a rock star was more demanding than I had anticipated. I also mentioned how it was healthy for me to return to my roots. "I need to come back to that, to my family and friends, to keep me from believing all that 'star' baloney," I said. "My feet are still on the ground. Any of my friends in Rochester, when I come back, they know it's me. There's no put-on. I'm a little more financially secure now, and I have a little more self-confidence in terms of telling someone to take a jump when I don't like what they are saying. But I don't have fine clothes or a long Cadillac. I just don't feel there's much of a change." I also talked about how fortunate I was that the Foreigner opportunity came along when it did. "I was having some serious second thoughts about my life," I told a reporter. "[After the accident that destroyed Black Sheep's equipment and cost them their record contract and the tour with KISS] I was ready to turn to just writing music. But just about that point I got the call from Mick. I'm sure luck had something to do with it. It could've been any one of the guys in Black Sheep. It was just luck they needed a singer and not, say, a guitarist."

As I prepared to take the stage that night at the old War Memorial, the butterflies were fluttering big time in my belly, and I couldn't help but flash back to that teenage moment when I defied my parents so I could see the Stones play back in 1965. I'll never forget the roar of the packed house of 10,200 fans when the lights flicked on and we began playing. The crowd was electric from the get-go, lighting sparklers, batting beach balls and balloons, and holding up signs welcoming me home. When we finished the first song, the audience serenaded me with chants of "Lou! Lou! Lou!"—chants they would repeat throughout the night. The fans were jacked up—maybe too much—because at one point some idiot threw a firecracker onto the stage and I felt like I jumped about 10' into the air when it exploded.

In his review in the *Rochester Democrat and Chronicle* two days later, Jack Garner, a nationally renowned film critic, sang my praises and captured the atmosphere.

"Lou Gramm was hoping for 'a triumphant return'—and that's what it was.

"The energetic singer bounded about like a man possessed, his long, curly mane flying behind him. Foreigner's music on record presents a balanced front—with no one element standing out—but in person, Gramm's incredibly powerful voice surges through the band's wall of sound and emerges as a startlingly rich element.

"Foreigner is a terribly loud band—one of the loudest around—and it would take an exceptionally strong singer to be heard at all. Gramm not only is heard, but he manages to find room amid the barrage for excellent phrasing, lovely tonal quality, and subtle nuances of inflection.

"Gramm has become a polished vocalist, already one of the best in rock today. His voice is the type that makes one believe he could sing anything in any style whenever he wanted."

We played for nearly two hours—and there was so much adrenaline coursing through me that night that I could have played six or seven hours. The crowd was so into it that it coaxed us into doing three encore songs. When I finished the final encore—a powerful rocker called "Headknocker"—I thanked the fans a final time and added, "I'll be back in town for a rest over the holidays—maybe we can get together for a beer." Before I could leave the stage, a representative from the mayor's office presented me with a city medallion (the equivalent of the key to the city), and the top-rated local radio station gave me a commemorative plaque.

Backstage, I was pumping more hands than a presidential candidate, signing autographs and posing for pictures until my eyes were seeing spots from all the flash bulbs going off. "I can't believe all this," I shouted above the celebratory din. "I'm ODing on all my friends." I then gathered together my parents and the band for a portrait shot. That was the best part of the night— seeing the parental pride on Ben and Nikki Grammatico's faces.

Foreigner would play in my hometown several more times through the years, and we would even do some rehearsal sessions there before the launch of one of our tours, but none of those concerts would ever top the first one. Who says you can't go home again?

After taking a few months off at the end of our American tour, we headed to England and played in front of an enthusiastic crowd in London that immediately seemed to respond to our music. Unfortunately, the critics didn't share the concert-goers' enthusiasm and tore us apart pretty good in the tabloids the next day. At first, Mick and Ian took the reviews extra hard because this was our first time performing on their home soil and they were hoping for a kind reception from the press. But we convinced our British bandmates that it was no big deal as long as the ultimate critics—the music fans—kept flocking to our concerts and the record stores. English music critics tended to be contrarians anyway; they like very little of what they review, so we had plenty of company in that regard. We sloughed it off.

Following London, we played shows in France, Belgium, Germany, Switzerland, and Italy before heading to the Far East, which included concerts in Hong Kong, Singapore, Kuala Lumpur, Australia, and New Zealand. The tour had been billed "Around the World in 42 Days," and it was both exhilarating and exhausting, but we were happy we had done it because it opened up a new door of opportunity. Foreigner was no longer foreign to international audiences. We truly had become a worldly band, and our music continues to be popular in Europe, Australia, and Japan all these years later.

While we were on our international tour, we learned that "Double Vision" had won a People's Choice award as song of the year. We were thrilled about the news, but unfortunately we were unable to get back to Hollywood for the ceremonies because of our tour commitments. Actor Erik Estrada, one of the stars of the popular late-1970s, early-1980s television show *CHiPs*, accepted on our behalf. To this day, I don't know why Estrada wound up pinch-hitting for us that night. Perhaps he was a fan of our music, or maybe the producers of the show wanted big stars to accept for those who couldn't be there to add to the glitz. During his acceptance speech, Estrada said something to the effect that he was accepting this on behalf of Mick Jones and Lou Gramm and, "If they think I'm giving this back, they're nuts." And sure enough, I never got the People's Choice award. Until, that is, nearly 33 years later. My wife, Robyn, and my current manager contacted someone from People's Choice and got a

replica of the crystal award I was supposed to receive back in
'79. It's one of the nicest gifts I've ever been given, and it took
me totally by surprise.

• • •

Our ascent had been meteoric, unprecedented, and as our record
sales proved, we had developed an enormous following in a short
span of time. But despite the brisk sales and rousing receptions
during concerts, not everyone was enamored with us. Music
critics were especially venomous, labeling us a "corporate arena
rock band." In their warped eyes, there was a formula to our
success devised by the record label executives. We supposedly
only wrote songs that would please our bosses and followed the
formula they had created for us. The criticism was baseless, total
BS. The way we composed our songs was no different than the
way any successful band composed songs. Ideas came from band
members and were thrown on the table. We'd bash them around
among ourselves, experiment playing them in our studios, and
hammer them into something respectable.

In retrospect, I think we were the victims of our rapid rise
out of nowhere. That really seemed to irk some critics who
believed we should have been playing clubs and dives for three or
four years before tasting success. The reality was that each of us
had done that individually, but we hadn't done that collectively,
so somehow our success was undeserved. It was a pretty flawed
and unfair premise, if you ask me. But we were only human,
and it did bother us. I think we eventually came to terms with
it. While *Rolling Stone* magazine was especially harsh, others,
such as *Billboard* magazine gave the band, and me in particular,
some positive reviews. It called me "a real find" and praised my
"outstanding vocals."

6

Less Is More

One of the negatives of the back-to-back tours was that it put us behind as far as coming up with new songs for a third album. Usually, we'd have three or four songs already written before we ended a tour, but not this time. That international tour knocked the hell out of us—physically and mentally. We spent our rare days off during that journey catching up on our sleep rather than writing and rehearsing.

My biggest problem with the tour was the time away from home. I felt tremendous guilt not being back in Westchester County with my wife, who was pregnant with our first child. There's no doubt that the guilt trip resulted in me drinking more heavily. It was no longer a case of having a casual drink or two to unwind; it was a case of drinking to get drunk in a foolish attempt to suppress those guilty feelings. And this was a problem that would only grow worse as we continued to pump out albums and spend months on the road promoting them with concerts.

As a result of that first international tour in the first few months of 1979, it took us longer to record *Head Games* than it did our first two albums combined. Our first album was produced by John Sinclair and Gary Lyons. They were an effective team and complemented one another well. One guy was more like a cheerleader; he was enthusiastic and vocal and would work hard at pumping you up and getting the best out of you. The other guy was more quiet but a very skilled musical engineer. John and Gary had experienced some success, but they were still up-and-comers in the business who, like us, were looking for that big breakthrough album. We had a good working relationship with them, and I think the result was an excellent-sounding album.

For our second album, Mick decided we needed a more prominent producer if we wanted to take the next big step forward, so he contracted Keith Olsen. Keith had just finished producing Fleetwood Mac's *Rumors* album, which was an enormous success, and I believe he had also done work for Toto. He was riding high, and we had to give him a much bigger cut than we had given Sinclair and Baker, but the money proved well-spent because the *Double Vision* album sounded fantastic thanks to Keith.

Mick figured we needed an even bigger name to produce our third album and hired Roy Thomas Baker, who had received critical acclaim for his work with Queen and the Cars. Sadly, neither Baker nor his engineer would live up to their gaudy reputations. Mick liked to contract a different producer for each album because, as he said, "One album isn't enough time for a producer to inflict his style on us." I also think Mick did it because he didn't want any producer to usurp any of his power.

After the tour ended in the spring of 1979, we took off for several weeks. The timing was impeccable for me because that

June my first child, Nick, was born in Westchester County. I couldn't have been more proud, and I was really looking forward to becoming a doting father, but those plans went awry when I received a call from Mick telling me that they were ready to start recording again—at a studio near his Southern California home. I was crushed because I figured we'd be working on our third album at our New York studio. Now he wanted me to leave my wife and newborn son for a few months. I was pissed. But I didn't have a choice, not if I wanted to continue pursuing this musical dream of mine, especially during this momentous but fragile time for a band on the rise. I looked into having my wife and Nick come with me, but he was literally a newborn and way too young to travel. My wife's sisters and mother wound up coming down from Rochester to help her out, giving her a solid support group she wouldn't have in L.A. So I packed my suitcase and my resentment, and I flew to the West Coast determined to work as rapidly as I could on this album so I could get back to my wife and our baby boy. Unfortunately, Mick and my bandmates didn't share my sense of urgency.

As I mentioned, Mick had contracted Baker to produce our third album, and we were extremely excited about that because Queen's albums sounded marvelous and Baker had a lot to do with that. We thought he would be a great fit and help us take that next big step up the ladder.

They put me up in the penthouse of a hotel. The accommodations were great, but I felt lonely and guilty not being with my wife and Nick. I phoned home every day, and it would break my heart when my wife told me that Nick had done this or that for the first time and I wasn't there to see it. There are no second chances to witness these milestones. It didn't help that Mick and a few other members had homes in the Hollywood Hills with their wives and families. The plan was to start working on our new songs each morning at about 10:00. Well, I showed up promptly at 10:00 that first day of rehearsals, and the rest of the group didn't show up until about 3:00 in the afternoon because they had been partying pretty hard the night before. This continued for several days, and the partying would continue during what were supposed to be recording sessions. It got to the point where before a note was even played, we'd go through two or three bottles of Dom Perignon or Taittinger champagne. I admit it, I imbibed right along with everyone else, and before you knew it we had the upper shelves of the studio lined with the bottles we had drained. We weren't even halfway through the album, and there wasn't any more room for bottles. So we'd take the bottles down and start all over again.

Compounding matters, Baker, the brilliant sound artist, stopped showing up regularly. His engineer would have to coordinate the recording sessions in his absence, and sometimes he would be so snockered that he couldn't even get up from his chair. There were many days when he wasn't there even when he was there. Not surprisingly, after a few weeks of these boozy recording sessions, we didn't have a single thing on tape worth listening to. We were spinning our wheels, and I was growing more angry and resentful by the minute because I was missing precious time with my kid. So one morning I'd had enough, and I caught a cab to LAX to fly home. The funny thing—or maybe sad thing—was that I had been back in Westchester for several days before they even realized I was gone. I finally received a call from Mick. He asked me why I had left, and I told him that we'd been at it for a couple of weeks and we didn't have anything to show for it because we had been more concerned with partying than making new music. I said I was as much at fault as anyone, but the time for having a good time needed to stop. We needed to get back to serious work or we were going to experience a dreaded decline and go the way of so many failed bands before us. I also expressed my displeasure about being away from my young family and if I had to be away, it damn well better be for something productive. Mick said he understood completely and that he would insist that we start working on the third album in earnest. I flew back to L.A., and this time we began some serious work on our third LP.

We had conceived what we felt were some good songs, but we had hoped Baker's genius for mixing sounds would elevate what we had to another level. That's what we hoped for, but Baker let us down. So as it turned out, we had to scramble to salvage the album and meet our deadline. I wasn't pleased with the finished product; there were distortions and other problems with the sounds. It sounded unfinished.

We released the title track, and "Head Games" briskly shot up the charts and did well for a while. Then the spit hit the fan. The lyrics—along with the risqué photo of a scantily clad teenage girl wiping her phone number off the side of a stall in a men's room—offended many. Before you knew it we were learning what the expression "Banned in Boston" was all about because stations there stopped playing our songs and called for record stores to remove the album from their shelves. The movement soon spread to other places, including the Bible Belt, and preachers were sermonizing against the album. I heard stories where they actually broke our albums in two in front of their congregations. We tried to explain in print and radio interviews that the song and cover were meant to be funny with a little edge, but our words didn't register with many. The controversy followed us through much of our tour in 1979.

There were some arenas along the way where picketers showed up to protest. Although *Head Games* sold well, its commercial success paled in comparison to *Foreigner* and *Double Vision*, selling about two million fewer albums. The controversy hurt us no doubt, but I think the poor production quality also had an impact. The songs and ideas were solid, but they weren't up to the level of the songs on the first two albums.

So after having been on this remarkable rise with our first two efforts, we fell a couple of notches. Some critics were writing that this decline might mark the beginning of the end. Although I thought that was being a little melodramatic, I was concerned. And apparently so were the executives at Atlantic Records who called a meeting to plot our future. They certainly weren't going to cut us loose. We had been too successful for that to happen, and they had been at this long enough to realize that even the best bands have a dip at some point. They believed that we could rebound and replicate the success we had with our first two albums. But we also knew that we probably only had one more shot at getting it right or they might entertain pulling the plug. By this point, I had become more heavily involved in Foreigner's decision-making process. And although Mick was still clearly the leader of the band, he sought my input on many things. We each realized that Foreigner was at a crossroads, and after several long and hard discussions, we decided that we needed to dramatically shake things up and remake the band.

We had already made one change before the *Head Games* album, replacing bass player Ed Gagliardi with Rick Wills, who had previously played for Roxy Music and The Small Faces. As I mentioned, Ed was obstinate at times, playing the song the way he wanted to play it rather than the way it was drawn up. Mick often had to stop sessions to get Ed back on track, and after a while it became tiresome and slowed down the recording process. Ed took the news really hard; he actually fainted after being told. Rick was a good replacement. He was a known musician who had played with Peter Frampton. He played simple and to the point, which is what we needed, and he was easy to get along with. I think we auditioned about 17 or 18 bass players before we came across him. Among those who applied for the job was one magnificent guitarist who had gained fame with a major band but had a serious cocaine addiction he couldn't kick.

During the summer of 1980, we started writing and recording a couple of songs for our fourth album, but neither Mick nor I were pleased. We'd listen to these rough working titles and say things like, "Well, it's pretty good. I like this part. I don't like that part." After a while we came to the conclusion that this stuff didn't sound any different from our last album, and it forced us to take a hard, honest look at the band. Our assessment—it was a decent band with good musicians and good guys, but something just wasn't right. A stodginess, a complacency had settled in, and we were at a point in the band's life where we couldn't afford that—not if we didn't want to become a defunct band. We knew that if we recorded an album similar to *Head Games*, we were done. Finished. Kaput. So we asked each other, "If it was up to you, what would you do?" And we reluctantly reached the same conclusion. We had to remake the band, cut it back from six to four, and fill in with session players in the studio and in concert.

In retrospect, I think the fact we had six guys in the band added a lot to the inner turmoil. The chemistry that made the band right in the beginning didn't necessarily mean it would always be right. I think a pretty major communication lapse appeared, and I don't think anybody really knew what anybody else was feeling—the deep, inner belief about the direction of the band and how we were progressing. We had reached a point where there was a lot of dissatisfaction.

I will never forget that September day in 1980 when we broke the news to the guys. We wanted to do it as gently as possible, but there is no easy way to fire someone. This wasn't some foolish reality show with Donald Trump. This was real life. And these were real people—friends and comrades who had helped each of us realize a dream. Everybody showed up at our New York studio that particular day with the idea that this was going to be like any other day—that we would be recording stuff for our fourth album. I had a sick feeling in the pit of my stomach as Mick and I began to speak. In a quavering voice I told the guys that we respected them as musicians and as friends and appreciated all of their contributions to the band. And then Mick told Ian McDonald and Al Greenwood that we had decided to let them go. They were clearly stunned and indignant. After absorbing the initial shock, they grabbed their stuff and swore at us as they stormed out of the room. It was one of the most unpleasant days I've experienced in the business.

Ian and Al were understandably angry and hurt, and they skewered us pretty good in a *Los Angeles Times* article headlined, "Foreigner Says Peace Was Foreign." We were portrayed as a band in turmoil, a band that had been on the verge of being torn asunder from internal strife. In separate interviews, Ian and Al described their dismissals as unnecessary and unfair. They said they both had suffered from creative frustration and said Foreigner had become a two-man band with Mick and I as the primary songwriters. "The rest of us were squeezed out," Ian said. "I found it hard to work under those conditions," Al added.

Top: My parents, Ben and Nikki Grammatico, met at one of Dad's big band concerts, and Mom later joined the band as a vocalist. They obviously passed along their love of music to me and my brothers. (Courtesy of Lou Gramm)

Left: That's Mom, Dad, big brother Ben, and me at a family outing. (Courtesy of Lou Gramm)

Here I am demonstrating my batting stance as a Rochester, New York, Little Leaguer. Baseball was my first love. I became a huge fan of the Brooklyn Dodgers and their graceful centerfielder, Duke Snider. Like many Dodgers fans, I switched my allegiances to the New York Mets after the National League club left Brooklyn for the West Coast. (Courtesy of Lou Gramm)

My yearbook photo from my senior year (1968) at Gates Chili High School in suburban Rochester. Dad thought my hair was too long. Imagine what he thought a few years later. (Courtesy of Lou Gramm)

Our band, Black Sheep, produced two albums for Capitol Records in the early 1970s. We were on our way to the big-time until a highway accident destroyed all of our equipment on our way home from opening for KISS in Boston on Christmas Eve 1975. (Courtesy of Lou Gramm)

I've had a fascination with muscle cars since I was a kid. That's me with one of my prized possessions—a 1965 Pontiac GTO. Our drag races up and down Lake Avenue in Rochester, New York, as teenagers inspired the Foreigner song, "Rev on the Red Line." (Courtesy of Lou Gramm)

Here I am striking a pose in our Manhattan recording studio while completing work on our first Foreigner album in 1977. (Photograph by Len DeLessio)

Loosening up my pipes while laying down tracks for that first Foreigner album. (Photograph by Len DeLessio)

The original Foreigner. From left to right: Ed Gagliardi, Mick Jones, Dennis Elliott, me, Ian McDonald, and Al Greenwood. (Photograph by Len DeLessio)

Once a drummer, always a drummer. I was a percussionist during my early music career. Never in a million years did I think I would become a lead vocalist. (Photograph by Len DeLessio)

There are few experiences that can compete with the emotions you feel during a live performance. I try to put my heart and soul into my music each time I take the stage. (Courtesy of Lou Gramm).

Belting out the ballad, "I Want to Know What Love Is," with a gospel choir backing me at a charity function in Beverly Hills in 2010. (Photograph by Tim Crozier)

In 2011, my alma mater—Gates Chili High School—inducted me into its alumni hall of fame, and I gladly returned to speak to the students about pursuing your dreams. (Courtesy of Lou Gramm)

"I felt castrated, cut off from everything." Mick responded by relating how he felt Ian and Al had become complacent during the making of the *Head Games* album and how that complacency carried over into the subsequent tours. It was not a pleasant experience having our dirty laundry aired in that story, and it only heightened the pressure we felt to get our musical mojo back.

Atlantic Records president Jerry Greenberg, who had been a great believer in us from the start and was so instrumental in our early success, reluctantly signed off on our decision to pare things down, but he also made it perfectly clear that our changes had better result in a much more successful fourth album, or else. The onus was clearly on Mick and me. We immediately went to work on writing new songs, finding a new producer, and lining up some session players. Despite the increased pressure, Mick and I believed that we could turn this thing around. We knew it was Foreigner's only hope. Status quo would have been our death knell. We needed to shake things up, not only with the personnel but with our music. As I told a reporter, "We were either due to assert ourselves at the very top of the rock pantheon or pack it in. This [departure of Ian and Al] was emotionally wrenching for us. It really took a lot of guts. It also meant that now the rest of us had to shine."

Mick agreed with me that we needed to find a producer who would provoke us to step outside our comfort zone. We found such a man in Robert John "Mutt" Lange. He was a Zambian-born British producer who had worked with AC/DC and Def Leppard on several best-selling albums, and he was a guy very much in demand. We heard that he could be a little bit on the pushy side, but that was okay; that was what we needed. We found out that he had just finished an AC/DC album and had a short window—six or seven months—in which to work with us. That meant we'd really have to crank, but we felt it was worth the opportunity to work with him. Lange told us to start playing as a trio—guitar, bass, and drum—and then bring in keyboard players that could hear the song and come up with a sound that would complement it. The main guy we brought in was Thomas Dolby, who played keyboards and synthesizers. His work is all over our fourth album, particularly in the signature synth sound for "Urgent." Dolby is a brilliant guy, and I really enjoyed watching him work. He's one of those quirky creative types—kind of weird almost, but a lot of fun to be around.

We went at it full-bore, and I could sense things coming together. I was feeling an energy I hadn't felt since that first album, and I believed that not only were we bouncing back but that we were creating our best stuff yet. It was a very exciting time, but it was also a very trying time, too, because we could feel the meter running. After a year into it, we still weren't done. Compounding matters, we had gone through our entire budget. All of that keyboard stuff we were experimenting with had elongated the process. So we asked Bud if he could have John Koladner from Atlantic Records come down to the studio and listen to the several songs we had finished so he could get an idea of just how innovative this album was going to be. He liked it a lot, and then we told him that we were just a few songs short and asked if Atlantic could extend our budget a few more months so we could wrap it up. He grudgingly agreed, and we adopted a schedule that had us working 16–18 hours a day, seven days a week.

Like I said, the keyboard stuff made this a more tedious journey. But the vocals were also more involved. Part of it had to do with some creative differences between Mutt Lange and me. Some of the vocals he wanted me to do sounded like Def

Leppard and some of them sounded like AC/DC—too much like them. So I would have to stand my ground and sing it so it sounded like me and like Foreigner. I know that miffed him at times, but we were intent on remaining true to our own sound and not copy someone else's. "He's a musician and a fine singer himself," I told a reporter when asked about Lange. "And he was on my case from the moment I walked into that studio. Lange likes the screamer approach. Hey, I like to scream with the best of them, but not all the time."

We finally got the album done, but before we did the final mixes, Mutt had to return to his work with AC/DC. I think Mick and I were able to do a pretty good job with it, and we couldn't wait for its release in July 1981 because we believed we had compiled something special, our best work by far. The execs at Atlantic felt the same way. Album covers back in those pre-Internet download days were an important part of the sales equation. We saw that with *Head Games* in a somewhat negative way when that risqué photo of the teenage girl resulted in a backlash against us. Rather than name the new LP after one of our songs, we decided to simply call the album *4*—a double entendre playing off the ideas that it was our fourth record and the group now consisted of four members. The artwork was inspired by the old newsreel clips that were once played in movie theaters. Before a film would come on you would see this countdown from 10 to zero, with numbers flashing on the screen. We had the No. 4 frozen and placed on our cover. It was simple but very sharp-looking; my favorite cover of all the albums I've done.

The promotional people at Atlantic Records put together a solid album launch publicity campaign. We didn't pull any punches in the press kit that was sent to the radio stations and music critics. "In rock 'n' roll, as in everything else, the only real constant is change—hit today, gone tomorrow," our publicist wrote. "Having sold close to sixteen million records worldwide—and monopolized the Top Five for months at a time with the albums *Foreigner*, *Double Vision*, and *Head Games*, as well as singles like 'Hot Blooded' and 'Cold as Ice'—Foreigner is not about to go away."

The release acknowledged the dramatic changes we had made both in personnel and in our musical approach. "This one's gonna blow the lid off," I was quoted as saying. "We've got something to prove again." Mick echoed my enthusiasm, saying this was the beginning of a new era for Foreigner. "Things became a little too comfortable, and people became a little bit jaded and blasé about things," he said. "I feel that what was coming off our records was becoming a bit predictable. This new album came out of a desire to get back the fire, the excitement that made the band in the first place." Near the end of the release I summed up my feelings with these words: "The pressures of success are to get you to duplicate or maintain what you've already done. We don't have that attitude. The growth of the band musically is what's important." I agreed with Mick that we needed to get the fire back, and I was confident the long days we had put in on this album were going to pay off with our best work yet.

• • •

We decided to release the single "Urgent" to drum up interest in the album. The song had special meaning to us because there was a sense of urgency about the band's future. And it had a great, great sound. It's obviously built around a fabulous guitar riff by Mick, but it was also made memorable by the wailing saxophone solo by Junior Walker. It's an interesting story how that came about. We hadn't quite finished the music to "Urgent." It was almost there, but it needed something more and we couldn't quite put our fingers on what that more was. We were browsing the *Village Voice* newspaper one day when we came across a blurb saying Walker was going to be playing at one of the clubs in the Village. Sirens—or in this case—saxes went off in our heads. That's what this song needs to finish it off—a sax presence. I was busy that night, but Mick and a couple of the guys decided to go see Walker play with the idea of asking if he would make a guest appearance on our album. When Walker was done with his gig, they approached his son who was the drummer in Walker's band. They told him they were from the band Foreigner, and he said, "Yeah, yeah," even though it was apparent he had never heard of us. Mick mentioned how we were working on this really cool song and that we'd love to have his dad come to our studio and record a track for it.

They didn't mean that night, but that's how Walker interpreted it. So they took him to our studio at about 3:00 in the morning. I guess at first he was playing some soulful, soft stuff and Mick went up to him and asked if he could really start honking in the manner of a rousing song, like Road Runner. "Oh, you want the loud stuff," Walker said. "I can do that if you'd like." So for a good 10–15 minutes, Junior wailed away the way that only Junior could. He finished about four takes, looked at his watch, put his sax away, and put on his hat. One of our engineers asked Junior if he could play another take, and Junior politely declined and said, "I think you got what you need," before he walked out the door. As it turned out, they had recorded a great beginning on one of the takes, a real honking middle on another, and very cool ending on one of the other takes. So the engineers were able to cut and splice, and they just made the pieces fall where they wanted them to fall. And the result was one of the most memorable sax riffs in the history of rock 'n' roll.

Here's a neat addendum to that story. Months later, when we were playing the Los Angeles Forum, Junior came onstage and played the song live with us and brought down the house. It was the only time he did that, and I'll never forget it.

"Urgent" proved to be a great lead-off hitter, climbing all the way to No. 4 shortly after its release in June 1981. It opened the door for three other chart-toppers—"Juke Box Hero," "Waiting for a Girl Like You," and "Night Life." While the AM stations played those four songs to the hilt, the FM stations played every—and I'm not exaggerating—every other cut from the album. Our pre-release premonition that we had something special with this album proved resoundingly true. Not only did 4 become our fourth platinum album within a month of its release, it became the top-selling album of 1981, beating out Pat Benatar's *Precious Time*, Stevie Nicks' *Bella Donna*, Journey's *Escape*, and *Long Distance Voyager* by The Moody Blues. Our album also did well internationally, finishing fourth in Germany and fifth in the United Kingdom.

I was especially pleased with the success of "Juke Box Hero," which peaked at No. 26. I wrote most of it, and it was definitely autobiographical, inspired by my formative years in Rochester when I would drum along to Beatles songs in my basement and dream of one day becoming an artist whose pulsating music roared out of juke boxes everywhere. The song talks about a kid waiting outside the arena of a sold-out concert for which he didn't have a ticket. I was that kid. There were many times I would hitchhike to the old Rochester War Memorial in hopes of meeting someone who might have an extra ticket. And if I couldn't find one, I would go to the back of the auditorium and literally put my ear against a metal door so I could hear the music. Every so often, one of the security guards would open the door and feel pity on me and let me sneak in. But there were many concerts when that didn't happen. I'd be outside that back door, standing in the rain while Jimi Hendrix or Vanilla Fudge did their thing. And that was okay. As the music and the roar of the crowd penetrated that back door, I would fantasize about being on stage, playing that one guitar while belting out tunes in front of a huge throng of adoring fans. I realize that I was hardly alone in my rock 'n' roll fantasy. So many young people from my generation dreamed the same dream, which is why that song really resonated with them. Mick did a superb job with the guitar riffs. I loved singing "Juke Box Hero"—still do.

"Waiting for a Girl Like You" was our ballad offering—a change of pace from our hard-rock songs—and it gave me a chance to showcase my voice. You won't believe how many guys—and girls—have come up to me through the years and told me how they slow-danced and made out to this song. The ladies, in particular, seem to love it. The song was Mick's idea, but I had a lot of input. We decided to use a chorus for background, and Dolby added the synthesizers. I was really pleased with how it turned out. It wound up climbing to No. 2 on the singles chart, and it held on to that spot for 10 weeks, setting a Billboard record for the longest run in the second slot without becoming top dog. We were hoping it would crack No. 1, but it just missed out.

During what would turn out to be my final recording session of "Waiting for a Girl Like You," this gorgeous dark-haired woman—an absolute knockout—walked into the control room and plopped herself down in the front row of theater seats near the glass that looks out into the studio where I was singing. I figured she was someone Mick and Rick knew, and to be honest,

I couldn't take my eyes off her because she was so stunning. I begin serenading her as if she were the girl I'd been waiting for all my life. I gave it my all for about 45 minutes, and just as I finished my final take, she smiled at me, waved good-bye, and walked out of the control room. Like a teenage boy with raging hormones, I walked into the control room and immediately asked, "Who was that?" The guys looked at me funny. "What do you mean?" Mick said. "We thought she was somebody you knew." We all started acting giddy, barged out of the room, and jogged down the hallway in search of this mystery woman. We never did track her down, and to this day I have no idea who she was. All I know is that she inspired me to hit all the right notes for that ballad. I have never sung that song better than I did that day.

One other song from that album that was special to me was "Luanne," a Buddy Holly–style rocker named after an old friend of mine from Rochester.

We promoted 4 by embarking on our most ambitious tour ever—North American and international jaunts that began on September 11, 1981, and lasted about a year. Our domestic tour ran for three months and featured sellouts in 51 cities in 28 states and Canada. During that time our album not only ascended to No. 1 on the charts, it also earned quintuple platinum status with five million U.S. sales. In April 1982, we began our European leg and quickly discovered that our international following was bigger and more passionate than ever. We were greeted with standing ovations at sold-out shows throughout England, Scotland, Belgium, France, and Germany, and the sales of 4 earned it gold, silver, or platinum certifications in Europe as well as Israel and South Africa. In late May, we returned triumphantly to the states for another domestic leg of the tour that ran through

August. The receptions and the album sales continued to be astounding.

Highlights from our travels included a magnificent photo safari through a game preserve in South Africa and a concert in Munich in which Jimmy Page and Robert Plant joined us on stage for a rocking rendition of "Lucille" during an encore. It was very emotional for Page and Plant because it was the first time they had been together on stage since the death of fellow Led Zeppelin bandmate and drummer John "The Beast" Bonham two years earlier. It was cool for me to share the stage with Plant because I had always admired his reckless singing style, and some critics had compared my three-octave vocal range and stage presence to Plant's, which I took as a high compliment.

The huge enthusiastic crowds we played for seemed to enjoy not only our music but also the high-tech staging, swirling lights, and 15' inflatable juke box that we pulled out near the end of each show. Personally, one of the most gratifying things about the album and the tour was that I was finally beginning to win over even my harshest rock critics. Among them was *Toronto Globe and Mail* music critic Liam Lacey, who wrote:

"The principal thing that Foreigner still has going for it is singer Lou Gramm, who sings in a hoarse scream that sometimes sounds like Roger Daltrey and sometimes like Led Zeppelin's Robert Plant. It's a powerful rock and roll instrument, and Gramm has the ability to put enough juice into even a nothing song to make it sound compelling."

Another critic was even more effusive:

"Lead vocalist Lou Gramm shows he's working his way out from under the shadow of Led Zeppelin's Robert Plant. He's trying for some new vocal sounds, much the way Bruce

Springsteen did in 'Hungry Heart'…he seems to be headed for a more distinctive style that can only help him in the long run."

Our decision to remake the band had been a risky one, but it had worked out fabulously. Spurred on by four Top 40 singles, 4 spent 10 of its 81 weeks on the best-selling albums chart at the top spot, selling more than six million copies. As if that weren't enough, Atlantic Records released a greatest hits album called *Records* just before Christmas 1982 that climbed all the way to No. 1 on the best-seller lists and became our fifth top 10 album in five attempts. That was pretty remarkable when you think of it. Only five years in the business and we had already produced enough hits to merit a "best of" LP that would become a seven-time platinum album. Our first eight singles had cracked the Billboard Top 20 (with four breaking into the Top 10), making us the first group since the Beatles to achieve that feat. We had become a rock 'n' roll phenomenon, and we believed that we hadn't yet peaked—not by a long shot. As I told a reporter at the time, "There are some chances taken. It's a satisfying progression for me, although I wouldn't want to stop there and tread water, that's for sure. I see this album as the first in a series of progressions."

7

I Want to Know What Foreigner's Future Is

When we finally returned from our domestic and international tours promoting 4 near the end of 1982, we were emotionally, physically, and mentally spent. The last thing any of us wanted was to be cooped up in a studio and attempt to write and record new material any time soon. Atlantic Records executives were thrilled with our unprecedented track record and understood our reluctance to return to the studio for a while. They plotted out a different strategy for us in the interim. Rather than worry about recording, they wanted us to embark on another mega tour later that year. The thinking was that we had assembled a deep reservoir of hits and we should ride that wave for as long as we could, then go back to recording. As a result, we went almost three years before releasing our next album—*Agent Provocateur*—in December 1984.

Our only other studio work was producing a soundtrack for the 1984 Summer Olympics. We were one of several artists asked to contribute a song to the soundtrack for the Games that were being held that summer in Los Angeles. The organizers had assembled a mix of eclectic music acts and they wanted us to do an instrumental, which was kind of strange, given that we had never done instrumentals before. We wound up producing a song titled "Street Thunder," which was brassy and majestic, kind of a victory song.

After recuperating from the exhaustion of the 4 world tour, we did head back to England to work briefly with trendy British producer Trevor Horn. He persuaded us to try to record our next album there, but it didn't work out. We quickly discovered that Trevor was more interested in keeping an eye on his English bands, like Frankie Goes to Hollywood, than in working with us. It wound up being a waste of our time and money and we headed back to the United States and spun our wheels for the next few years.

One of the huge downsides of being a successful recording artist is that you're always dealing with the question, "What's next? What's next? What's next?" There isn't a whole lot of time to savor things, to catch your breath, to rest on your laurels. You have to keep feeding the monster you've created, keep cranking out the hits. It took a long while for us to recharge our batteries, and when we did get back to creating new music, it became apparent that the dynamics had changed.

When Mick and I finally resumed writing, I began worrying about the direction the band was headed. We had carved out an identity as a hard-rock band, and now it appeared that Mick was intent on softening us with more ballads and less edge. We had ended 4 with a real soft song, "Waiting for a Girl Like You," which was a commercial success. And now Mick was talking about launching our fifth album with another ballad, "I Want to Know What Love Is."

At one point, I told him that I wasn't comfortable with this philosophically, that we were selling our souls. It was a sentiment shared by our bass guitarist, Rick Wills. Mick didn't seem to care. He just dismissed our concerns. "Man, you've got to go with the flow," he told me. "It's a new world out there, and we've got to adjust to it. We still have this rock song and that rock song." I told him, "Mick, come on now. The care and time we spent on 'Urgent,' 'Juke Box Hero,' etc., are now being spent on ballads. Don't get me wrong. 'Waiting For a Girl Like You' is a great song—a really great song—but it was set up by the great rock songs we produced. Is this the direction we're headed because if it is, I'd like to know because we're doing irreparable damage to our rock image."

He started to get very defensive. He said all bands go through phases, and this was a phase we were going through. I told him that was bull, that we ran the risk of losing our fan base if we made such a dramatic move. The more I tried to make my case, the more I realized I was banging my head against the wall. I could see that he had made a major decision about the future direction of Foreigner without my input. In retrospect, this was a turning point in our relationship. The collaboration and the give-and-take so essential to our success up to this point would slowly give way to his dictates. Gradually, it would become his way or the highway. The dreaded catch-all music phrase—creative differences—eventually came into play, and we would experience our own Lennon-McCartney, Jagger-Richards split.

• • •

Mick was fluent in French and had spent a chunk of his career in Paris, which was the genesis for the catchy title, *Agent Provocateur*. I liked the phrase a lot because it implied a spy-like figure who was planted to provoke havoc. Unfortunately, the music we produced on that album, though successful, didn't create the kind of havoc we had with 4 and our previous albums.

Mick was especially excited about, "I Want to Know What Love Is," and although it was his idea and he did a lot of the work on the song, I devoted a lot of time to it and made some tweaks here and there that helped bring out the soulfulness. Having a gospel choir sing background vocals was a stroke of genius, and it happened purely by chance. We were working on the song in the studio when an acquaintance of Mick's, who represented a small gospel label, stopped by. He and Mick shook hands and hugged, and he asked if he could watch us rehearse. After Mick and I finished, the man pulled us aside and said, "I don't know if you would like this idea or not, but I'm just going to throw it out there. This song would cross over several genres if you could put a big soulful gospel choir behind it, sort of like Edwin Hawkins did on the song, 'Oh, Happy Day,'" which was an eighteenth-century hymn that became a top-five hit. We knew immediately what he was suggesting, and we said, "Wow! That just might be the missing piece we've been looking for." He told us that he had just the right choir that could pull this off.

A few days later members of the New Jersey Mass Choir joined us in the studio, and I can see the scene like it was yesterday. Just before they were to sing the chorus, they gathered in a circle and held hands while reciting The Lord's Prayer. Once they began singing, the hair rose on the back of my neck and goosebumps sprouted on my arms. I mean, when they opened their mouths it was like a choir of angels—very emotional.

It wasn't practical for the New Jersey Mass Choir to tour with us because it would have taken the singers away from their jobs or school obligations. Singing was a hobby, not a career for them. Plus, it would have been cost-prohibitive for our band to foot the cost of having 25–30 additional people traveling with us. So instead we decided to recruit choirs in cities where we'd be playing. We hired a woman, Margaret Taylor, to line up the backup singers for "I Want to Know What Love Is" in advance of our concerts. She had been a singer herself and had been a production assistant with the Jacksons, so she was eminently qualified for the job. She would often contact churches or the music departments at colleges and universities. In exchange for the choir's services, Foreigner would donate some money to the choir or its sponsoring organization, such as a church or a music department. The singers in the choir were usually thrilled to tears to be able to perform the song with us. You could see the nervous excitement in their eyes as they prepared to join us on stage in front of 10,000–20,000 people—audiences often 100 times larger than any they had performed in front of before. After booking the choir, Margaret would send their director a tape of the song along with sheet music and instructions, and we would hold a quick rehearsal the day of the concert. There were several occasions where she wasn't able to line up a choir. In those cases, we would either recruit members of our warm-up band or ask the audience to fill in as our chorus.

"I Want to Know What Love Is" was clearly a singer's song—a song that allowed me to show off the full range and resonance of my voice. I loved singing it, and I loved the fact it shot to the top of the charts, becoming our first No. 1 song. What I didn't like were the artistic ramifications. Like I said, our hit before "I Want to Know What Love Is" had also been a ballad, and I believed that the juxtaposition of the two power ballads was tearing us from our rock 'n' roll moorings.

• • •

We were in the final stages of recording *Agent Provocateur* in the early part of 1984 when this young guy named Bryan Adams came into our studio. He told us he was recording in a studio down the hall and had a dilemma. This was the last day he had booked the studio for, so he had no choice but to finish his recording that day or his album would be delayed, perhaps for months. Apparently a couple of his vocalists had taken ill, and he needed someone to sing back-up vocals. I could see he was desperate, so I volunteered to help him out. I wound up singing in five or six of his songs, including his signature single, "Cuts Like a Knife." He was so grateful and offered to pay me, but I told him it wasn't necessary. He was so appreciative that he gave me credits on the album. I'm sure he would have done the same for me. It was just a case of one rocker helping another as far as I was concerned. And it's something I've tried to do whenever I could throughout my career, including those times when I backed-up for Aerosmith and for Don Mancuso, my longtime Rochester friend and bandmate, on his *D: Drive* album.

Agent Provocateur was a commercial success, selling more than three million copies to earn multiple-platinum status. And I was happy that one of our rockers from the album—"That Was Yesterday"—had success, peaking at No. 12 on the singles charts. But the recording artist in me was very worried that we had turned the corner and were venturing down a road that would lead to our ruination.

Once we completed an album, Mick and I would sit down and figure out the royalty ratio for each song. We'd come up with a percentage based on what each individual contributed to the lyrics, the melody, and the editing of the song. And we'd also determine writing credits, which for virtually every song ended up being both Mick and me. It was usually a pretty painless process. For our first three albums, each session probably lasted about 10 minutes max. Things began to change, however, during the negotiations for 4. Although I had contributed almost equally to "Urgent," Mick didn't want to give me credit. We haggled about it for a while before he got his way. I wasn't real thrilled about the agreement. And from that point on, I didn't trust Mick. My negotiations with him would never go smoothly again.

Our negotiations reached a nadir when it came time to divvy up money and credit for the songs on our *Agent Provocateur* album. We had developed a system where he and I would get together—just the two of us—and write down what percentage we felt we had contributed to each song. We then would exchange the folded scraps of paper and verbally hash things out. "I hope this isn't going to be difficult," Mick said when we sat down in the break room of our studio in late 1984 to decide who got what from our fifth LP. As it turned it out, it was very difficult, with little agreement on any of the songs.

When it came time to determine the percentages for "I Want to Know What Love Is," I wrote down "Mick 60; me 40." He wrote down what he thought was fair on his sheet, and we exchanged the scraps of paper. When he unfolded my sheet, he immediately became indignant. I then looked at his sheet and read in disbelief, "Me 95, Lou 5." I was pissed beyond belief. "Are you for [bleep]ing real with this?" "Not only for [bleep] ing real," he shot back. "I'm being generous." I wanted to leap across the table and strangle him. We jawed back and forth, back and forth, back and forth, but he wouldn't budge. He was firm on his 95–5 split. "Mick, we spent weeks working together on this song, and I made contributions that went way beyond five percent," I said. "If you want to humiliate me by offering me five percent, then I'll give you what you fucking want. You can have it all, you SOB."

His hard-line stance cost me millions of dollars, but beyond that it had sent a powerful message to me that I was no longer a serious partner in this band. It's was Mick's band. And I was about to be reduced to nothing more than a bit player, a vocalist, a conduit out there to do things the way he demanded. From that day forward, I would have less and less of a say in Foreigner's direction and less and less input in the songwriting process. The working relationship we had forged through the years wasn't working any more.

• • •

Whenever I was super stressed about things, I would try to spend some extra time at my brood farm near my home in rural Westchester County. I first became captivated by horses after we had moved to the suburbs in the early 1960s. When I was about 12 we would go to a nearby farm that was owned by one of my brother Ben's friends. We would be there almost every weekend in the summer, and Ben and I would help out the young kids who came there to ride horses for the first time. We'd assist them getting onto the horse and situated in the saddle, then lead the horses around by the reins for about 15 minutes at a time. The kids would feel safe because we had control of the horses, and it gave us a chance to get to know the various personalities of these beautiful animals. I loved working with the horses and seeing the looks of astonishment on the kids' faces. And when we were through being guides, we'd climb aboard and go riding ourselves, sometimes for hours.

We had about six or seven mares on the ranch I purchased in the early 1980s, which I got for a great price. It was what you called a farmette—a small farm—and it featured about 11 acres of pasture land. I was able to hire a couple of people who were horse experts. My interest was in breeding Western horses for competitions such as barrel racing and other events that you often see at county and state fairs. We would transport our mares to particular farms in the Midwest where they would be sired with horses that had been accomplished competitors so that the foals' lineage would be unquestioned.

Several of the horses we raised went on to do well in competitions. It was a horse we didn't sire, but rather bought and nurtured, that became our highest achiever. I can still see her plain as day. She was a palomino named Stella Dallas Star. I had chosen that name after the 1937 movie in which Barbara Stanwyck plays a self-sacrificing mother. Stella Dallas was a well-trained horse that we brought from obscurity. She wound up winning several prestigious events and at one time was ranked fifth nationally. I still have one of her trophies adorned with red, white, and blue ribbons. It's a prized possession and a reminder of a happy time in my life.

I reluctantly sold the farm and the horses around 1987, about a year before I moved back to Rochester. It was very difficult to part with the horses because I had become so attached to each of them. They're such smart, beautiful animals. They really do become part of your family. I think about them from time to time—very fond memories.

• • •

Our American tour in 1985—our first in three years—included two memorable stops in Rochester—one good, one not-so-good. We played the sold-out War Memorial on May 12, and the old hockey barn was really rocking. The crowd of 10,000 serenaded me with chants of "Lou! Lou! Lou!" throughout the night. Between sets, the deputy mayor presented me with an official city medallion, just like he had done during my first Foreigner concert there seven years earlier. But the highlight of the night occurred when the Mount Olivet Baptist Church Mass Choir came onto the stage to sing the chorus for "I Want to Know What Love Is." They did a superb job, and I loved seeing the expressions of joy on their faces while they were swaying to the music. After pounding out "Urgent," we bowed to the crowd and then bounded off the stage, only to be summoned back for an encore by the roaring throng. I quickly pulled on a Gates Chili High School soccer T-shirt before returning to sing "Dirty White Boy," "Hot Blooded," and "Juke Box Hero." During that final song, this huge inflatable juke box rose from the back of the stage. Kind of hokey, but the concert-goers loved it. It was a magnificent evening.

Our return trip, roughly three months later, was not so magnificent. Blame it on the weather and a flight delay. The promoters had booked us to bat cleanup that late August day in a four-band outdoor concert at Rochester's Silver Stadium. More than 19,000 people showed up at the old minor league baseball park on Norton Street, and the promoters had put together a pretty good lineup that included Steven Tyler and Aerosmith. Unfortunately, Mother Nature didn't cooperate as a steady drizzle put a damper on things. The inclement weather had the crowd in a less-than-festive mood, and the fans became even more ornery when they had to wait 90 minutes between Aerosmith's final set and our first one. I was already in Rochester and ready to go at our scheduled time, but the rest of Foreigner had been delayed flying out of Westchester County Airport. Some concert-goers tried to make light of the delay and began taking running slides through the puddles that had formed on the tarp covering the infield. (That didn't please the general manager of the Red Wings ballclub. He was concerned somebody might get hurt and the club might get sued. He was also worried that the infield was going to be ruined by the weight of all the fans on the diamond.)

As the crowd's impatience grew, some angry fans began wadding up paper cups and throwing them onto the stage. Fortunately, the plane carrying my bandmates arrived at the airport, the police escorted them immediately to Silver Stadium, and we were able to defuse a potentially nasty situation. I forget which song we opened with, but it had to be a rocker. Unfortunately, it didn't get much response from the audience, so I bellowed into my microphone, "Why are you people so quiet?" They finally got into it when we began playing "Urgent." Later on, we encountered another glitch when the local choir that was supposed to sing the background chorus for "I Want to Know What Love Is" didn't show up. We improvised by recruiting backstage personnel, family members, and musicians from the three other bands to form a makeshift choir. It all worked out, but it wasn't our finest hour in my hometown.

• • •

Mick and I had been a fairly prolific writing duo, but that changed as he disappeared for long stretches of time following our tour to promote *Agent Provocateur*. It would be three years before we released our next album, *Inside Information*. That LP featured two top six singles—"Say You Will" and "I Don't Want to Live Without You." And the album earned platinum status, peaking at No. 15 on the charts. But it also reflected that we were on the decline in terms of popularity. For the first time, one of our albums had failed to finish among the top-five sellers.

Other than vocals, I contributed very little to *Inside Information*. Mick had already chosen the song ideas, and there was little or no room for contribution. Working for Foreigner had become just that—work. I would basically show up, sing the songs, and put on my hat and coat and leave. I was punching the clock, just like I had done so many years ago when I was working in a furniture store in Rochester. Making music with Mick and Foreigner was no longer my passion; it was my job. I was miserable because I no longer felt I was contributing anything significant other than my pipes. Creatively, I had been locked in a cage. My vocals were on *Inside Information*, but my soul wasn't. I definitely felt as if my days with Foreigner were coming to an end. And to be honest with you, I couldn't wait. I was anticipating it like a man about to be unshackled.

When they launched *Inside Information*, I told Mick I wouldn't be touring to promote the album because I had no input in its production. Mick was enraged, but I didn't care. My attorney had scoured my contract and saw nothing in it that required me to tour. Bud Prager, our manager, called me and asked me to reconsider. I said, "Bud, I've spoken to you on numerous occasions while this album was being recorded and told you about my misgivings. This album is not a Foreigner album. This is a Mick Jones album. This is the direction he wants to go. This isn't a group effort. Artistically, I was given crumbs. I was basically shut out of being a creative member of this band, so I see no reason to promote. I don't even like the finished product. I feel no connection with it at all." I eventually calmed down and did some concerts, but the tour was nothing like the tours Foreigner had been accustomed to, either in scope or duration. The excitement we had generated with our early albums was continuing to wane. I just didn't like this new easy-listening rock group that we had become.

There's a funny story regarding that soft-rock approach we had taken. One of the songs from *Inside Information* was the ballad "I Don't Want to Live Without You." Mick was all excited about it, but I thought it stunk to the point that I didn't even want to sing it. So when it came time to record it, I under-sang it—no little twirls, no passion, no Lou Gramm vibe to it. And wouldn't you know it, despite my efforts to sabotage the blasted song, it shot all the way up the charts to No. 5. Sheesh!

• • •

The idea of recording a solo album had been percolating in my mind for many years, and I would mention it from time to time to the guys in the band. But we had been way too busy recording and touring for me to find the time or the energy to really pursue it. Plus, there were some restrictions in my contract with Foreigner that prohibited me from going solo. The fear was that I would wind up being in competition with the band.

I finally saw an opportunity after we finished touring to promote *Agent Provocateur* in late 1985. We had our obligatory three- or four-week break, then we were supposed to start writing and doing our pre-recording work on our next album. But that's when Mick announced that he was going to take a vacation with his wife to Europe for about three months. I decided to use that time to work on some solo stuff, including a good, hooky, commercial rock song I had co-written with Bruce Turgon called "Midnight Blue." I thought it was a catchy song, and I even offered it up to Mick so that we'd have at least one memorable rocker on the upcoming album. Bruce lived in Sacramento at the time, and he came down to Los Angeles so that we could play the song for Mick and the guys. There's a really compelling guitar riff at the beginning—the kind that Mick really excels at—so I asked him to play it and he did, but he played it as flat as a board. I go, "Whoa, Mick, that's not the way it's meant to be played." He said, "It's not?" So Bruce came over to him and showed him how it should be played, and Mick said, "Okay, I see what you are doing," then he proceeded to play it the same lifeless way he played it the first time. It immediately dawned on me that he was playing it that way because he had no interest in recording the song for Foreigner, so that was that.

But I knew the song had great potential, and if Mick wasn't interested, then screw him, I'd use it for my own album. The problem, though, would be to find a guitarist able to do the piece justice. We were practicing it one day with the band that was recording my solo album, and I put on a Nils Lofgren song to demonstrate what I was looking for. I can't remember who connected me, but before the day was over, I was on the phone with Nils himself, telling him what a huge fan I was and asking him if he would be interested in helping me out with "Midnight Blue." Lofgren, who gained fame for his solo stuff and for his work with Bruce Springsteen and the E Street Band, said he'd be happy to, and I'll be forever grateful because he really gave "Midnight Blue" the uniqueness that set the song apart. Nils is what I call a guitarist's guitarist. He's really superb. Many, many years later, in the summer of 2011, he called to see if I would do backup vocals on his new album, and I was more than happy to return the favor.

I've mentioned about how you often stumble onto lyrics and titles for songs. Well, the same is true for melodies and riffs. That's what happened with "Midnight Blue." I was not a proficient guitarist, but one day I was fooling around with my six-string and I happened upon a basic version of the riff we used. I was much better on the piano than guitar, so I immediately went to my Wurlitzer piano and began expanding on the chord pattern. It wasn't exactly there but when I played the piano version for Bruce Turgon, he immediately picked up his guitar and started playing what he had heard. "Do you mean this?" he asked after strumming for about 10 seconds. "I do mean that," I said elatedly. Those are the wonderful creative moments for a songwriter, when the thought of a distinctive sound you hadn't heard before and only conceptualized becomes reality.

• • •

Mick's three-month vacation was followed by several months of producing other bands' albums, including Van Halen's *5150*—their first album with Sammy Hagar replacing David Lee Roth as lead singer. Foreigner was clearly in limbo, and that was fine with me because that downtime from the band during the summer of 1986 gave me plenty of time to work on my first solo album, which I titled *Ready or Not*—as in ready or not world, here I come. My intent was to get back to my raw, gritty, garage-band roots, to rediscover that sense of spontaneity that Foreigner had lost because of Mick's insistence on polishing and burnishing every freaking note.

I scheduled a meeting with several executives at Atlantic, including the president, Doug Morris, and told them that Foreigner was moving in the wrong direction musically as evidenced by our last album, which had done okay but wasn't nearly as successful as our previous efforts. I also mentioned that for about a year I had been telling Mick we needed to get back to what had got us here, but my advice kept falling on deaf ears. I then handed them the demos I had done on "Midnight Blue" and the proposed title track "Ready or Not" and told them that Mick didn't care for them but that I thought they would make a good foundation for a solo album. They listened to the demos and were enthused, giving me a budget to produce the album.

We launched the album in 1987 by releasing "Midnight Blue," which rocketed up the charts to No. 5. Not only did it achieve sales success, it also became the most-played song on the radio that year, even beating out U2's signature song, "Still Haven't Found What I'm Looking For." By the time Mick finally came back—after six months instead of three—I had finished 90 percent of the album. He gathered members of Foreigner together and said, "Let's get started on a new album." I told him I was finishing up my album, and he just brushed it off in typical Mick fashion, saying, "I know. Just finish it up, have them put it out there, and be done with it." I said, "Mick, the first thing I learned from you is when you release an album, you better be ready to promote it. Well, I have a tour lined up." He just laughed. "So you've got some clubs lined up that you are going to play," he said snarkily. I told him, "No, I have a full-fledged tour, where I'm going to open for the Steve Miller Band." All of a sudden, the blood began rushing to his head. I knew what was coming next. He'd always had a difficult time controlling his temper, and he was ready to start screaming at me. But he knew he wasn't going to change my mind, so he just stormed out of the room.

I knew I had ruffled some feathers with him and other members of the band. And that became a focal point of reporters' questions when I went out to promote the album in the first few months of 1987. In many people's minds, I had a lot of explaining to do. "At this point, the situation is very, very touchy," I said in one of my newspaper interviews that February. "There may be a little bit of resentment, some feelings of betrayal. There are a few bruised egos involved." But I actually believed the album would be beneficial to the band, too. "I feel more resigned to my role within Foreigner now that I have an outlet for my other ideas," I said in the interview. "I feel more at peace with my image."

"For me, it was about trying to do things that would never be tried with Foreigner," I continued, "because there's a format that Foreigner songs took, a roundabout way to getting to the hook or just building that song dynamically. Just because of Foreigner hits in the past, certain songs had to go through a process to become Foreigner songs. I don't particularly subscribe to that. I like things to be a lot more immediate and to the point, certainly a lot more stripped down."

The critics seemed to pick up on what I was saying. One, who liked *Ready or Not* a lot, summed it up well. "There are 10 songs on the album—nary a one that flaunts the extended song intros, keyboard pomp, or repetitive choruses that have sold millions of records and won the scorn of critics. This album gets out from under the layers of studio sheen and over-dubbing that typified Mick Jones' approach to production."

In an interview with the *Rochester Times-Union*'s Steve Dollar, I elaborated on this point. "I think the spontaneity factor is one which wasn't really dwelled upon in Foreigner…where on my album I really went for performance and damn the mistakes. There were not a lot of overdubs. I wouldn't say the record is comprised of first takes; they are flawed to a certain degree. But the sincerity and conviction is there, and they get across the sense of recklessness I wanted."

I went on to say that the process works really well for Foreigner but that it wasn't my approach and that I went to great pains to make sure the record didn't sound like Foreigner. "I wanted to avoid all obvious comparisons," I said in another interview. "I did songs I couldn't do on Foreigner albums.

Some of these songs were offered to Foreigner but didn't get any attention. In other words, the songs on this album weren't Foreigner-ized. I know all about that style. There's a slow buildup of the chorus, full-blown productions, long drawn-out song intros, certain harmony patterns. It's easy to avoid. In my songs, I prefer getting to the point rather than drawing out the suspense. Foreigner songs sound more controlled and stylized. I pulled the plug on the synthesizers, cut down on the overdubs, and kept the contents blunt and direct. I wanted to avoid ballads on my album. I want my rock credibility back."

I was able to pull together a solid studio band to record the album. In addition to Lofgren's magnificent guitar playing, I relied on Turgon to help in the writing of eight of the 10 songs. I also had him contribute musically with the bass and rhythm guitar tracks as well as some lead guitar and keyboards. I got my longtime friend and Black Sheep alumnus Don Mancuso to help out with some guitar riffs. I enlisted my older brother Ben, who had worked with Yoko Ono and Peter Frampton, to play the drums, and I got my younger brother to play a couple of guitar tracks.

But the most memorable Grammatico contribution actually came from an unlikely source—my dad. I convinced him (without much prodding at all) to play a trumpet solo on the song, "She's Got to Know." Other trumpet sounds on that song were produced by Crispin Cioe and Mark Rivera from the Upton Horns, a Rochester-based group that my father played for. Although some might accuse me of nepotism, all of my relatives and my dad's friends were accomplished musicians. Each of them nailed it, and I couldn't have been more pleased than if I had hired the most famous musicians in the world. That Dad was able to be part of it was an extra bonus for me.

And I think it might have fulfilled a little bit of a dream for him, knowing that his horn blowing would be preserved forever on a record album. I know he thought I was pulling his leg when I first asked him to participate.

As I said, Atlantic Records arranged for us to tour with the Steve Miller Band in June 1987, and I wasn't sure how that would work out because there was a stark contrast between our styles of music. But as had been the case with the odd pairing of the Doobie Brothers and Foreigner, the audiences embraced both bands despite the differences. I got to know Steve during that tour and found out he is a fantastic guy. He and his bandmates were terrific people to work with.

The pairing of bands is always an interesting dynamic. You never know how it's going to work. And sometimes the thing blows up right away, not because of a clash of musical styles but because of a clash of personalities. I'll never forget the time we had Billy Squier open one of our U.S. tours. I think it was after the first or second show that Billy started hitting on Mick's wife. She told him to get lost, but Billy was too ripped to pick up on the fact that A) she was married, and B) she wasn't interested. Well, Mick showed up at the post-concert party and saw what was happening and came close to punching Billy's lights out. Needless to say, that kind of set the tone for the tour. Everybody was walking on eggshells after that.

• • •

Thanks to the pervasive radio play we received and the tour, *Ready or Not* was a commercial success, achieving a No. 27 ranking among the year's best-selling albums. But beyond that, it had revived my creative juices and got me thinking more and more about breaking away from Foreigner and the oppressive atmosphere micro-managing Mick had created. The solo experience was liberating. And yes, I'd be lying if I didn't tell you that it felt good, damn good, that an idea of mine—"Midnight Blue"—an idea that had been trashed by Mick, had ended up becoming the most listened-to song in the United States in 1987.

The album helped me return to my rock 'n' roll roots. As I told a reporter, at age 36, "I'm not particularly after a middle-of-the-road crowd. I'm not ready for Vegas or to be cast in the role of a balladeer. I'm after the kid who likes good hard rock, a borderline metalhead. I don't think I'm too old for that."

It's funny, but in spite of all the success I had achieved, there was still a part of me that felt unfulfilled as a musician. "I've never actually reached the dreams I set out to go after," I told the *Rochester Times-Union* in a 1987 interview. "I'm still chasing what I'm after. I still think I have a lot to prove."

I believe that unfulfilled sense was rooted in what had happened—or rather what didn't happen—to Black Sheep. "Ten or 12 years ago when Black Sheep was together, we were going after something," I continued in that same interview. "I feel as if that's still unfinished business. I'm not saying this first album is the consummation of that. That's just step one."

I was clearly looking ahead to a future that might not include Foreigner when I concluded that interview by saying, "I've been with the band for 10 years. It's routine for me. Mick's behind the wheel, and I ride shotgun. I think my priority now lies with my solo career. I'd like to do an album a year or every 18 months. I'd like to just chisel out a place for myself in the scheme of things."

At virtually every tour stop I made while promoting *Ready or Not*, I was deluged with questions about my future with Foreigner. It really bothered me that Mick and Co. were resentful of me and the success of my solo efforts. "My album's reception has proven to be a disrupting factor," I told the *Los Angeles Times*.

"I think they're viewing this as kind of a betrayal. They're just not approaching it with a positive attitude, and they would like to put a lid on my album for the sake of Foreigner. I just won't have anything to do with that. So we're at an impasse, and I think they might be looking for a new singer."

• • •

To further sate my creative appetite, I asked my agent to search for any opportunities where I could write songs for movies or television shows, or where one of my existing songs could be used. Before *Ready or Not* was released, he came to me with a movie song possibility. Director Joel Schumacher was looking for music for the soundtrack for his teen horror film, *The Lost Boys*.

The timing was perfect for me because we had been working on a bunch of songs for our album and had a backlog of ideas. I had this one melody that I hadn't been able to develop lyrics for, but the concept of the movie script inspired me to break through my writer's block and conceive the words for "Lost in the Shadows." It came together rather quickly, and I sent it off to Schumacher. He really liked it a lot, as did Kiefer Sutherland and several other members of the cast. In fact, Schumacher was so thrilled with it he made it the title track and asked if he could come to town with a crew and shoot a three-to-four-minute film of me singing the song. It actually turned out being a much more elaborate production than I had expected. They had me dressed in tight jeans, boots, and a black leather jacket like one of the characters from the movie. And they also brought along some of the supporting cast, costumes, and pieces from the movie set. It took two full days to shoot and gave me an appreciation of how much goes into making a film. Schumacher even invited me to the Hollywood premiere of *Lost Boys*, and it was so cool to be able to hear part of my song in the beginning and then the

entire song during this motorcycle chase scene in the middle
of the movie.

I had done a few videos before for MTV, and I usually
enjoyed them. One of the more memorable ones involved our
song, "I Want to Know What Love Is." Mick and I are shown in
various scenes in deep thought, pondering the meaning of love.
When it reaches the point where I'm singing the lyric, "In my
mind, I've known heartache and pain…" these stage doors burst
open and members from a black gospel choir come streaming
in and belt out the chorus lines as we exchange handshakes
and high fives.

MTV videos were pretty primitive when they started out in
the early 1980s. The first ones basically just showed the musicians
on stage performing at a concert. But as time went on, the videos
became more and more sophisticated, almost like short films.
Aspiring movie producers, and even some established ones,
saw this as another creative outlet in which to tell a story, and
they would try to out-do one another. In retrospect, I actually
liked the early videos better because they reminded me of the
old black-and-white films of the Beatles and the Stones from
television shows like *Ready Steady Go!* The danger with the MTV
videos was that as they evolved, the director's and producer's
personality shaped your musical image, which could be incredibly
dangerous. MTV and its impact was a double-edged sword. For
bands that came out with mediocre songs, the videos enhanced
the longevity and importance of the songs. Then there were
bands—and I'm not going to name names—that were better
off not being seen, bands that weren't telegenic but played really
good music. In those cases, no matter how good the video was,
it wound up damaging the song.

MTV wasn't born until after we had released our first four albums, so we missed out on some excellent opportunities to plug the majority of our greatest hits. When we did finally appear on the network, we received gigantic boosts. They were almost like free three-minute commercials for our songs. MTV really did revolutionize the industry. Fans couldn't wait to see what visual story the Hollywood producers would concoct for each hit song. It wasn't until our fifth album that the MTV videos started to take off. You can still catch some of the old ones on YouTube.

VH1's *Behind the Music* was big back then. The episodes were like mini-documentaries produced by MTV's sister channel, and they attempted to provide viewers with an unvarnished, controversial backstage look at musical artists. Ours aired in 2002 and I thought it was, for the most part, honest and accurate. It gave us our due as influential and successful artists, and it delved into the tensions caused by Mick's overbearing nature. It also addressed my brain tumor and my arduous recovery. The mini-doc ended on kind of a high note, intimating that things were great between Mick and me, when in reality they were not.

• • •

The spring of 1987 was an incredibly busy time for me. During the day, I would go to Foreigner's Manhattan studio to lay down tracks for the *Inside Information* album Foreigner released later that year. Then in the evenings I would spend several hours rehearsing for my upcoming solo tour with Steve Miller. I could definitely feel a chill in the air from Mick and my Foreigner bandmates at those recording sessions. I had already said that I wouldn't be available to tour with the band until I was finished with my solo tour, and that obviously didn't go over well. While publicizing *Ready or Not* that summer, I made sure to let people know that I was still a member of Foreigner. "There might have been some backlash against me if the kids thought I was no longer part of Foreigner," I told a reporter from the *Toronto Star*. "I'm pleased to be doing one more album with them, but whether there's a long-term future for me in Foreigner…we'll just have to take it as it comes. But it won't deter me from my solo career."

I also reiterated how my album was distinct from the band's current approach, which I'm sure caused Mick's blood pressure to rise. "I think the arrangements [on *Ready or Not*] are much more immediate and blunt," I said. "I don't think my songs take on the epic kind of proportion that Foreigner songs do. I like the production stark rather than submerging it in a backwash of synthesizers."

Like I said, the North American tour with Steve Miller that June through August was a rousing success, and I'll always be grateful to Steve for allowing me to tag along to promote my work. He is a class act.

8

Taking Steps Down the Road to Redemption

I moved back to Rochester in 1988 so that we could be closer to my parents and in-laws. There was a time early in my career with Foreigner when I thought I had outgrown my hometown, which, between the city and surrounding suburbs, has about a million residents. I once vowed never to return, making some comments to reporters that I later regretted. I honestly believed back in the late 1970s that in order to be successful you had to be in the rock 'n' roll meccas—New York or Los Angeles. And because Foreigner's headquarters were in Manhattan, I felt obligated to live nearby. But the reality was that I was never going to be a big-city, bright-lights guy; I was basically a small-town boy with small-town sensibilities.

For me, Rochester has everything a larger city has to offer, just a little less of it. There's an intense sub-culture there that really loves music and the arts. And there's a great sense of community. People know one another and help out one

another. I describe it as a mini-metropolis. There's no doubt
that Rochester clearly has influenced my artistry. The way I
was raised and the experiences I had during my formative years
there shows up in my music time and time again. Looking back,
I spent 12 years living in the greater New York area, but it was
never home. Rochester was home. Absence made my heart grow
fonder, and I understood that Rochester was the place I needed
to return to in order to regain control of my life.

Late that year, I bought a building in downtown Rochester
that I turned into a recording studio for my solo band. I also
purchased a house and the lot across the street. My hope was
not only to have a place for us to record, but also to lure some
young and up-and-coming groups to record there, as well. And
I tried to encourage some veteran bands looking for an out-
of-the-way place to record where they wouldn't be bothered
by the distractions and exorbitant fees of a big city to come to
Rochester. Visiting artists would be able to stay in that house
across the street dirt cheap, and it wouldn't feel like they were
cooped up in a hotel. I also planned on using the studio to record
commercial jingles. I had big plans in hopes that Rochester
might become more of a music hub. Sadly, several years later the
city declared eminent domain and claimed my property across
the street. I fought it long and hard, but they said they were
going to use the land to build an apartment complex. A dozen
years later, nothing has been built. After razing that house, the
property became an empty lot and remains one. Please don't
get me started on politicians and the games they play.

On May 14, 1988, I experienced one of the most memorable
nights of my career. In celebration of its 40th anniversary, Atlantic
Records scheduled a huge 13-hour reunion concert at Madison
Square Garden, and Foreigner was one of the featured artists. At

the suggestion of Atlantic's producers, we used singers from the assembled bands instead of our usual gospel choir to provide backup vocals when we performed "I Want to Know What Love Is." I will never forget the scene for as long as I live. I was out there on the stage, belting out the lyrics when I turned around and there was Phil Collins on one side of me and Jimmy Page on the other. Several other stars soon joined in. It was absolutely electric.

• • •

I continued to sing what I was told to sing for Foreigner, but I had little if any say in the creation or writing of the songs. I was no longer a co-leader of the band, just a set of vocal chords, a conduit for Mick's ideas. And so I did the minimum I was required to do for Foreigner while I focused my creative energies on my second solo album—*Long Hard Look*—which was released by Atlantic Records in 1989 and featured two top 40 hits "Just Between You and Me" and "True Blue Love." "Just Between You and Me" climbed all the way to No. 6 and underscored that I still had it as a songwriter if I was just given the opportunity. I collaborated on the song with Holly Knight, who came up with the chords. At that point, I was single again and the lyrics spoke to something that I longed for in my life. *Long Hard Look*, which peaked at No. 85 on the best-seller list, came out around the same time as Mick's solo album—and his record bombed despite the contributions of backing musicians such as Billy Joel, Ian Hunter, Joe Lynn Turner, and Ian Lloyd.

I made a few attempts to sit down with Mick and hash things out, to no avail. He would attempt to be diplomatic, but he wound up being condescending. He wouldn't say my songs weren't good; instead he would tell me that he didn't think they were up to the level they should be for Foreigner. After more than a decade of being a team, he made me feel as if I were an upstart auditioning for an opportunity. It was time to leave. My attorney found an "out" in my contract, and in late May 1990 I took it.

"It would have been nice to make it work, like Phil Collins and Genesis," I told a reporter after the breakup. "But I just felt like we'd always be at odds with each other because I couldn't give 100 percent of me 100 percent of the time...I don't have to feel guilty about my solo career when I don't have time for Foreigner. It's a tremendous weight off my shoulders."

Mick wasn't pleased, later telling a reporter, "I felt a bit jilted, a bit betrayed."

I didn't care in the least how he felt because I was finally out from under his thumb and free to pursue a brave new world. I knew there was risk involved, but I was confident venturing out on my own after two fairly successful solo albums. And there was something about the fear that comes with starting anew that appealed to me, made me come alive. I was going to stay solo, but then the opportunity arose to form a new band. Vivian Campbell, a renowned guitarist for Whitesnake and Thin Lizzy, was available; his only condition was that the group not be the Lou Gramm band but rather a collaborative effort, and I was fine with that. Bruce Turgon, who had worked with me in Black Sheep and on my solo albums, was also game, and the three of us, along with drummer Kevin Valentine (Donnie Iris and the Cruisers, Cinderella) formed a band called Shadow King. The name was inspired by what I had endured in recent years with Mick, namely that I had spent too much time in the shadow of a man who perceived himself to be a member of rock royalty. Shadow King released a self-titled album that was produced by Keith Olsen, who had produced Foreigner's *Double Vision* album many years earlier. Unfortunately, Keith was going through a messy divorce when he was helping us produce the Shadow King album, and the result showed in our finished—or should I say unfinished—product.

• • •

By this time it had become pretty apparent to me that my alcohol and drug addictions were taking a huge toll. My marriage, damaged by too many hours away from home, had dissolved, and I turned increasingly to other pleasures. My addiction became so fierce that I actually couldn't wait to get out of the studio or off the stage so I could get my high on cocaine and vodka, which proved to be a very volatile mixture.

I had sought help a few times in the past, going to rehab places for a week or two at a time, but they didn't really teach you how to address your addiction. There would be daily talks about alcohol and drugs, but it wasn't the main focus. They would emphasize eating the right foods, getting your sleep, and detoxifying your body. But they didn't really get to the core of why you were abusing drugs. They didn't really help you set up a support network to cope with a problem that would be with you for the rest of your life. I'd leave there feeling somewhat healthy and rejuvenated but would suffer relapses. One time I left the place and headed to the airport, and before I even boarded the plane, I found a bar and start pounding the booze.

In the fall of 1991, I had finally reached my wit's end. I had grown sick and tired of being tired and sick. I wanted, in the worst way, to pick up the shattered pieces and regain control of my life and repair—if possible—the damage I had done to my wife and sons. When my kids were younger, I could be hungover or strung-out and still fake them out with a false happy demeanor. But now they were 12 and 7—ages where I couldn't fool them anymore. They were now giving me funny looks that asked, "What the heck is going on with you, Dad? Why do you keep doing this to yourself?"

I had begun to do some research to find a place that specialized in addiction, and the more I read about the Hazelden Treatment Center in Minnesota, the more convinced I became that it was the place for me. After 12 destructive years, I was finally going to own up to things. This wasn't going to be like so many other times where I had sobered up for a week and then began scrambling to find that bottle of vodka and those lines of cocaine.

I know this is hardly earth-shattering stop-the-presses news, but a culture of addiction exists in rock 'n' roll. I think there are a lot of reasons for this, ranging from excessive fame and fortune, often at an early age, to the extreme loneliness and boredom of the road. I think touring can really take its toll. You're often spending your entire day cooped up in a bus going from one city to the next. You pull into a city a few hours before the show, do the show, party your ass off, then board the bus as the sun rises and head for your next destination. You're usually so revved up for hours after performing that you can't get to sleep. And you get into a pattern where you really cut loose after a show. I remember going into Mick's suite after concerts and there were be enough scotch and vodka to stock a liquor store, and you'd start imbibing. You'd be hanging out, talking, doing this and doing that, and then you would open the drapes and see this piercing sunlight and look at the clock and see that it was 7:00, 8:00, or 9:00 AM and realize that you needed to hop in the shower because the bus would be leaving soon.

Before long that became your daily routine, your unhealthy lifestyle. I can actually remember shows where my mind would start wandering, where I couldn't wait to get the concert finished so we could get to the party. In retrospect, it's amazing that I and so many of my rock 'n' roll peers were able to survive the abuse we put our bodies, minds, and souls through.

As I discovered, the path to sobriety is a precarious, complex journey. You obviously want to purge yourself of something that has been so destructive and has had such a grip on you. But in the deep recesses of your mind, you wonder if you will mourn the loss of this old friend that has been by your side for years. I know this sounds sick, but you actually find yourself wondering if your life is going to become quite boring without this crutch. Of course, the yearning for true health far outweighs everything else. You know things are going to be better for you, for your loved ones, and for everyone you encounter. You will no longer have to hide things and live a lie. Yes, that initial high of drugs and booze can be very, very attractive, but it's not worth the wrecked and trashed feeling you have the next morning. Nor is it worth the cumulative toll it exacts from you.

My moment of truth arrived in November 1991. I had just played a concert in New York and when the music ended, the party began. It was all there—anything an alcoholic and drug addict wanted. The buzz buffet line included top-shelf booze, cocaine, marijuana, hashish—you name it, it was available. I wound up being so gone I don't even remember what I imbibed or smoked or snorted that night. All I know is that I stumbled into my hotel room at about 5:00 AM totally disgusted with myself. I really believed I was going to die—not necessarily that day but in the coming weeks or months if I continued down this path. As I mentioned, I had sobered up before—once for as long as three months, but I always returned to my crutch. This morning, though, was different. I was fed up with myself, disgusted about being that person who used drugs and booze as an excuse for just about everything. I remember bawling my eyes out and dropping to my knees and begging God for help. "Please, Lord, please! Please help me change and stop being this despicable person!" After several minutes, I composed myself and dialed my attorney and told him to cancel my flight back to Rochester and book me for Hazelden. He said he would get on it right away but warned me that it usually took several days to process patients. Fortunately, within a half hour to 45 minutes, he called back and told me he had booked me a flight from New York to Minnesota and that there would be a car and a person from Hazelden waiting for me at the airport.

On that plane ride, I had a sense that my life was about to change forever—at least I hoped it was—but I also knew that I could never totally undo the damage I had done not so much to me, but to my wife and boys. I felt tremendous guilt and remorse about that, still do. There's a 12-year stretch that I wish I could do over without the booze and drugs.

I told only my closest relatives where I was going. The folks at Hazelden, like those who run and operate the Betty Ford Clinic, are used to dealing with celebrities and are good at maintaining a person's privacy, but that was the least of my worries. I was just concerned about getting well. Everybody is treated the same there, and I liked that. I wasn't Lou Gramm, Juke Box Hero, I was simply Lou Gramm, a flawed human being trying to kick his addiction to alcohol and drugs. The instant you arrive, you are greeted warmly and taken to the admissions office for orientation. While you are answering questions, security guards do a strip search of you and painstakingly inspect all of your belongings. It may sound extreme, but the last thing they want is for an addict to be doing drugs on campus. They want to make sure you haven't brought your "friend" with you. You are then assigned a dormitory room with several other men and given chores to do. It's a 30-day program, and for the first two weeks you have no contact with the outside world.

On your first full day, you go to a discussion group, introduce yourself, and tell people why you are there. It really is like what you've heard: "I'm Lou and I'm an alcoholic and a drug addict, and this is my story." It is a very emotional experience as you bare your soul. But I also found it to be very cathartic. You feel extremely fragile, but with each group session and each one-on-one counseling session, I began to feel more comfortable and began to understand why I had made the bad decisions I had made. It helped tremendously being among people from all walks of life who were in the same leaky boat as me. Although it was painful, it helped hearing others tell their stories about how they had allowed their drug usage to ruin their careers and their relationships. It made you feel that you weren't alone.

During the group sessions, you would usually talk for about five to 10 minutes, and then the group leader and your peers would ask questions or relate similar stories. My path to addiction didn't really start until my mid-twenties. Oh, I had smoked pot on a couple of occasions and had gotten drunk a few times before then, but it didn't become a problem until I joined Foreigner and Mick and I started spending late nights at his New York apartment collaborating on songs. I was introduced to cocaine as the deadline pressures for our first album intensified. I actually saw the benefit of coke—or at least the perceived benefit—because it would keep you awake and hyper alert, which enabled us to work deep into the night. It just took off from there and became not merely a part of my life but eventually a ruling force.

After a few sessions, I began to bond with other people at Hazelden. I came to realize how booze and drugs can be an equal-opportunity destroyer. I heard stories from others in the group that literally scared the crap out of me. There was a commercial airline pilot in our group who told stories about how he would fly from here to there and the minute he landed in a certain city, he and his fellow pilots and flight attendants would make a beeline for their hotel bar, drink until closing time, then go up to their rooms and do blow and smoke pot until the sun came up. Then they'd take their showers and drink their five cups of coffee and head back to the airport and fly a plane filled with passengers to some other destination. After years of doing this, he was about to fly another plane hungover and strung-out. When he pulled the plane into position to takeoff, he had a nervous breakdown. They had to pull the airliner back to the gate, and he finally sought help.

They would bring in speakers—esteemed people from all walks of life—and they would relate their battles with addiction and how they had finally regained control of their lives. It gave you hope that you could do it, too, even though it wasn't going to be easy.

While at Hazelden, I began to undergo a spiritual transformation. I met with a pastor there, and we talked frequently. I felt very comfortable with him, and he helped talk me through the guilt and the remorse I was feeling. In one of our final sessions before I left the campus, I told him that I felt the presence of Jesus Christ and I wanted to turn over my life to the Lord. And the faith that came into my life clearly helped me, particularly in the months and years following my decision to sober up. I walked out of that rehab center feeling so much better about myself, but I knew it wasn't going to be easy to stay clean and avoid the temptations of booze and drugs. It was going to be a lifelong challenge, one that I would need to face every day. I'm grateful to tell you that as of this writing, I've been sober for 22 years.

A few months after I returned to Rochester, I received a call from Mick asking me to fly to Los Angeles to work on some outtakes for a domestic greatest hits compilation. A similar album, released by Atlantic Records, had sold more than 700,000 copies in Europe. That was very gratifying and made me feel that our work had endured the test of time. Mick also said he wanted to discuss the possibility of me rejoining Foreigner. I was somewhat skeptical about that ever happening and declined to fly to the West Coast at first. But he called me a few more times, and after talking some more with him and some people at Atlantic Records, I decided to meet with Mick to see if we couldn't work something out.

Johnny Edwards, the vocalist he had hired to replace me, had not been well received at all by Foreigner's longtime fans, as evidenced by the tepid sales of *Unusual Heat*, the album Mick had produced after I left. And my group, Shadow King, had flopped and disbanded, so the timing seemed right for reconciliation. But it would only work if Mick was willing to go back to the way it was when I was a true partner in the band. I emphasized that I wanted to contribute songs and give input that would be taken seriously and not automatically dismissed. I told him I wanted "creative equity" in the band. The strange thing is that Mick and I met in late April that year, just as the riots were raging in South Central L.A. My plane was actually rerouted from LAX to John Wayne Airport because some of the rioters were shooting at the planes. We met at the Sunset Marquis hotel in downtown and became sequestered there for our safety because the city was under martial law and no one was allowed on the streets for a few days. There were armed guards with rifles stationed on the roof of our hotel and nearby buildings. Talk about surreal.

I remember seeing a television clip of Rodney King, whose brutal beating by the police and the officers' subsequent acquittals had ignited the riots. There he was, standing in front of a phalanx of cameras, asking the L.A. community, "Can we all get along?" That was kind of the theme Mick was selling me, too—can we all get along? We talked about old times, where it went astray, where it went right, our lack of communication, our creative chemistry and tension. I reiterated my concerns about the direction of the band, how it was becoming a little too soft and cuddly. I expressed those worries to him on several occasions before and had always been met with anger and disdain. But this time he listened rather than argued. And I did the same. We talked for a long time, and he seemed genuine about his pledge to allow me to be a contributing partner rather than a silent one.

During our meetings, there was another huge issue I needed to address. And that centered on my new-found sobriety. I told him that I had no intention of being the person I had been before in terms of drugs and alcohol; I had worked too hard at this to allow it to fall apart. I said I wasn't going to be part of the party scene any more, and that I preferred not to be around it. He claimed that he had dried out, too, but I wasn't buying it. So I knew this was going to be a big, big test for me, to continue to just say no when those around me were saying yes.

Before I headed to the airport, we shook hands and I was a member of Foreigner once more. Mick and I decided that the best way to reintroduce the band was to add a few new songs to the greatest hits album we were about to unveil. We were back in the studio not long after that reconciliation, and it felt like the first time—very natural—just like it had back in the late 1970s and early '80s when we were writing exciting rock 'n' roll songs. The first single we finished was "Soul Doctor," a hard-rocking tune that some described as "a Dirty White Boy for the 1990s." We also came up with a ballad, "With Heaven on Our Side," which rocked harder and had more of a guitar presence than "I Want to Know What Love Is" and "Waiting for a Girl Like You." The third song we completed for the greatest hits album was another rocker called "Prisoner of Love."

The thing I liked about those sessions was that it felt like Mick had rediscovered his guitar and the great riffs that set Foreigner apart. It seemed to me that we were making attempts to get back to what we did best—producing full-throttle rock 'n' roll music. And Mick and I were getting along much better. He was less overbearing than he had been, and the lines of communication between us were definitely open. The album was also enhanced by the backup work of gifted artists like Sheryl Crow and Cheap Trick's Robin Zander.

As we had hoped, the sales for *The Very Best of Foreigner… and Beyond* in 1992 were brisk, and the album achieved double-platinum status. And the new singles, especially "Soul Doctor," received some decent air play. But we wouldn't know for sure if we were truly back until we played our stuff outside the studio, so we scheduled a 10-city mini-tour for that fall. Although we had once been billed as the kings of arena rock, we decided to play smaller venues for the most part this time around. Before our first show of the tour, in West Palm Beach, Florida, Mick and I hugged, said good luck to one another, then kicked into a rocking rendition of "Long, Long Way from Home." It was the first time we had played a concert together in almost five years, and it felt like we hadn't skipped a beat.

The concerts sold well enough to prompt us to extend the tour an extra month into January. That December, Mick and I made guest appearances on *Live With Regis and Kathie Lee*, where we played acoustic fragments of several songs. It was funny because we could see that Regis Philbin had no idea who we were or what our music sounded like. He sat there with Mick at the piano, like someone preparing to have a tooth pulled. But Kathie really got into it. She said she was a big fan or ours, and it showed. It was good publicity for our album because they were the king and queen of morning television. The next day of that New York swing, we appeared on shock-jock Howard Stern's nationally syndicated radio show. Talk about a night-and-day contrast. We made appearances on a bunch of shows through the years, including those breakfast concerts in New York. There had been talk of us playing Dick Clark's *American Bandstand*, but unfortunately that never panned out. That's a shame because I think it would have been an awesome experience to have performed in front of one of rock's most influential figures.

• • •

I wouldn't say our newly constituted band was on the straight and narrow as far as behavior was concerned, but at the beginning of the tour the guys were good about restricting their partying to the hotel rooms. We had an alcohol- and drug-free bus. And that made it a lot easier on me, but that's not to say I didn't struggle with it—because I did. There were moments when I would feel this tremendous urge to have a drink or light up a joint or try something much more potent, like cocaine or hash. But whenever I felt the temptation, I would read some of my favorite Bible passages or phone one of the friends I had made at Hazelden. During my last private talk with my counselors there, they had warned me that 80 percent of the people in rehab suffered a relapse within the first year. Fortunately, I wound up being among the 20 percent who didn't. And I couldn't have done it without my faith and several of the people who went through rehab with me and were just a phone call away.

I made a bunch of calls during vulnerable moments that year, and I received a lot of calls, too. After I made it past that first year, it started to get a little easier, but you realize that you can never let your guard down. It's a lifelong challenge, and addiction is an insidious disease that's always lurking nearby like a snake ready to strike. And what made it tougher was that the booze and drugs were always around me, readily available if I wanted to partake. It wasn't only there among some of my bandmates, but also out there, in front of me, in the concert crowds. I could smell the marijuana wafting through the air, and I could see the cups of beer and the whiskey flasks being emptied in copious amounts. I had never really noticed it before—or thought anything about it—because I was as high as they were. It all just seemed normal to me.

• • •

We released another collection of our best stuff, titled *Juke Box Heroes: The Best of Foreigner* in 1994, but later that year we finally stopped trying to rest on our laurels and produced our first new album in about eight years—*Mr. Moonlight*. Two things come immediately to mind when I think about that record—we recorded it on the hallowed rock 'n' roll grounds of Woodstock, New York, and it was our first non–Atlantic Records venture. (I couldn't blame Atlantic for wanting to go in a different direction because we hadn't done anything of note for them in a long time, and there were serious questions about the band's future.)

I was very pleased with *Mr. Moonlight* because we were getting back to our rock roots in hopes of retrieving our old audience. We had stripped things down to the lowest common denominator. *Agent Provocateur* and *Inside Information* were laden with synthesizers and stacks of guitars, and I think we alienated some of our fans as a result. We wanted this album to be as direct and unadorned and ungarnished as some of our earlier albums. I was optimistic that this album was going to get us back on track and become a huge success. In the press release promoting *Mr. Moonlight*, I was quoted as saying, "I always felt that Foreigner never quite lived up to our own expectations, but I think with this album we're taking a big step to where we want to be. I want this to be what it always should have been… and better than it ever was."

We managed to hook up with Rhythm Safari, a power label internationally but just a little boutique label in the States. *Mr. Moonlight* was released in November 1994 and did fairly well in the United Kingdom, finishing as the 59th best-selling album of the year. But it bombed in America after being released domestically on its own label—Generama—the following February. The problem was that Rhythm Safari, which had some success with some rap artists, didn't have a strong presence in North America and didn't do a very good job of marketing the album there. So we didn't get the radio airplay we needed for people to become familiar with our songs. This was apparent when we went on tour to promote the album in the States. We would play our new stuff and the crowds would be polite, but you could tell they were curbing their enthusiasm until we started cranking out our established hits. The reception was totally different when we went to play in Europe, Japan, and Australia. Our new stuff received rousing ovations there, and again, I think it had to do with Rhythm Safari's ability to get international radio airplay. It's too bad that the album wasn't properly marketed in the U.S. because I still believe *Mr. Moonlight* was one of the best albums we ever did. And the few critics who took the time to give the LP a good listen seemed to agree. One of them, Chuck Eddy of *Entertainment Weekly*, wrote, "Almost every track here is as magnificently produced and hookful as the filler on *Double Vision* or *4*."

Mick had been true to his word, and I had extensive input in the creation and production of *Mr. Moonlight* and in the reconfiguration of the band. We assembled a formidable lineup of backing musicians that included Bruce Turgon, who had worked with me for years on solo projects and had been a member of Black Sheep; and keyboardist Jeff Jacobs, who had worked with Mick when he was producing Billy Joel's award-winning, multi-platinum *Storm Front* album. That's not to say everything was perfect between us. Mick could still be domineering at times, but he did give me room to create some of the songs, and that made me feel good, like I was a true contributor again. I thought the album was strong lyrically. It wasn't about getting the girl and doing her inside-out; it had some depth and meaning about life's struggles. My Christian faith had certainly influenced some of my writing, but I regard *Mr. Moonlight* as more of a spiritual than a religious album. I was really gratified by the reception it received abroad. It's just too bad few people in the States ever really heard it. The album was also special to me personally because—although I didn't realize it at the time—it would be the last studio LP I would record with Foreigner.

• • •

Around this time, the music industry was beginning to undergo a cataclysmic change. As a result, it was becoming more and more difficult, if not next to impossible, for heritage bands like ours to get their new stuff on the air. Corporate conglomerates went on a feeding frenzy in the 1990s, buying up radio stations by the handful. And the suits in corporate offices began dictating the music that was played, taking the freedom away from the DJs who had a feel for the industry and their listenership that went well beyond a spreadsheet. With the rare exception of a mega artist like a Springsteen or a McCartney, corporate wanted only new artists. Foreigner and other bands from the 1970s and '80s were pretty much relegated to classic rock stations. I don't mean to sound like an ingrate. It was cool that they were playing our hits—and still are—but we didn't have a venue to introduce and showcase our new stuff.

When we were touring with *Mr. Moonlight*, we'd go to the newer rock stations, and they were all excited about interviewing us about our past rather than our present and future. They'd wind up playing 30 to 40 seconds of our new stuff, and we'd leave them a copy of our album in hopes they would continue to play songs from it in their entirety after we left. But they invariably didn't because they viewed us as a heritage band that was all done creatively and had nothing new to contribute to the music scene. Plus, they were under strict edicts from headquarters. Then we'd go to the classic rock stations in hopes that they would give our new stuff some play, and they would do the same thing—play the new songs for 30 to 40 seconds then put on our old standards.

Interestingly, when we toured in Europe, Japan, and Australia, the radio stations there weren't like that. They gave our new stuff plenty of play, which is why *Mr. Moonlight* sold better and drew raucous approval at concerts there. It was so, so frustrating. We wanted to continue to grow and reinvent ourselves as a band, but like so many groups from the '70s and '80s, we had hit a creative brick wall that we couldn't go through, over, under, or around.

9

Battling Back from Death's Doorstep

s I recounted at the beginning of the book, I began experiencing axe-splitting headaches, blurred vision, and short- and long-term memory loss toward the end of 1996 and early 1997. I thought I was stressed out and everything would take care of itself if I just got a little rest. I was in a state of denial for the longest time, refusing for several weeks to admit that my problems were becoming unmanageable.

"It was getting to the point where Lou wasn't remembering a lot of things," my then-fiancée told Jeff Spevak from the *Rochester Democrat and Chronicle*. "I'd get frustrated and say, 'You're not listening to me!' And Lou would say, 'I've got too many lyrics in my head, it's my age, blah, blah, blah, blah,' until he'd heard it from too many people. I feared the worst. I kind of had a feeling that he had a brain tumor because he was having a short-term memory problem. I had a friend with the same symptoms—her tumor was malignant, she's since passed away—and that's all I could relate to."

The day before Foreigner was scheduled to embark upon a concert tour of Japan, I finally stopped deluding myself and went to see a doctor about my condition. The MRI he ordered confirmed our worst fears. An egg-sized tumor was discovered in my brain, and I was told by a neurologist in Rochester that it was inoperable because of its location. Stunned, I phoned Mick in New York to break the news. "Are you sitting down?" I asked. "There isn't going to be any tour to Japan. I've been diagnosed with a brain tumor."

My doctors arranged for me to see a world-renowned neurologist in the Big Apple, and sadly, he reiterated what the neurologist in Rochester had said. The doctor essentially told me to get my stuff in order because I was going to die. And that's what I was preparing myself for until I stumbled upon that *20/20* television feature about Dr. Peter Black, who was doing revolutionary things with laser surgery.

I contacted him and was able to get in for surgery within a matter of days at Boston's Brigham and Women's Hospital. Although Dr. Black told me there was a good chance he could remove the tumor and that I would eventually return to a normal life, I was understandably nervous. At about 4:00 AM on a late April morning in 1997, they put the IVs in my arm and began wheeling me toward the operating room. Although I was scared, I also felt a certain serenity. Six years earlier I had made amends and had allowed Christ into my life, so I figured things were going to work out. Either I was going to be able to continue my life on Earth with my loved ones, or I was going to meet my eternal savior. I was deep in prayer as they administered the anesthesia. Although I was under for the operation, there would be times when Dr. Black would bring me back to semi-consciousness so he could ask me questions. I don't remember what they were, but I do remember giving him succinct answers. And then I would go back under again. The tumor's location, near my frontal lobe and parts of my optic nerve, made the surgery extremely tedious and painstaking.

When I came to in the post-op area at around 6:30-7:00 PM, Dr. Black spoke to me about how things had gone. I could see how exhausted he was; he looked like he had just been on stage for a 13-hour concert, which in a way he had. He told me that it had not been easy, but that the operation was successful. He told me how they had shaved my head to make way for a horseshoe-shaped incision on the right side. The skin was then peeled back, the skull bone was cut away, and a laser was used to burn off the tumor. Dr. Black said he had gotten almost all of it, but there was a little bit that was between the two lobes of the brain that he wasn't able to eradicate, so I would have to undergo radiation treatments for that once I had healed. He said that recovery could take several years. "We didn't set a broken arm here," he said. "This was complicated and dangerous brain surgery."

The other interesting thing Dr. Black told me is that the tumor wasn't the result of my self-abusive lifestyle, but it was something I was born with that hadn't really started growing at an alarming rate until I was in my forties. This really took me by surprise because I thought for sure the drinking, drugs, and poor eating and sleeping habits I had practiced for so long had caused my problem. But in reality, this ticking time bomb in my head was genetic and had been with me my entire life.

I was able to go home within a few days, but I had to go by car rather than plane because I wouldn't have been able to handle the cabin pressure. In the days and weeks following the operation, I looked like something out of a horror flick. My head was swollen to twice its size, and I was wrapped in this huge turban-like bandage that had to be changed periodically. The early going of my rehab remains pretty much a blur because I was on heavy pain medication and it was going to take time for my brain to heal and for my memory and other cognitive functions to return to their previous states. They put me on steroids at first. I administered shots to myself every night, sometimes twice a night. I also took about 10 or 12 pills a day, plus massive doses of vitamins. I spent a lot of time in bed, sleeping and watching TV. I'd watch shows and not retain much. My brain, like an atrophied muscle, was going to need plenty of exercise before returning to full strength.

Several months after the surgery, I was back at Brigham & Women's Hospital for 30 straight days of radiation treatments. I had rented a nearby apartment, and my brothers spent time with me because I wasn't able to fend for myself and I was too exhausted to do much of anything. I had no appetite at that point. All I wanted to do was sleep. I'd be zonked out 18 to 20 hours a day. On those occasions where I did have some energy, my brothers would take me to the Quincy Market and I'd walk for 15 to 20 minutes before having to take a break. I would wear a knit hat pulled down low over my swollen noggin. I didn't have to worry about anybody recognizing me because I didn't look like me.

Once I finished the treatments, which were quite intense, we returned to Rochester, and slowly—very slowly—I began regaining my strength. Unfortunately, the surgery and radiation treatments had destroyed my pituitary and adrenal glands, and that turned my metabolism inside out. The pituitary regulates the body's hormones. When damaged—or in this case, destroyed—your body can be fooled into thinking it needs more food than necessary in order to survive. Not only did it cause me to eat more, but the food I did consume was immediately stored as fat. It was almost like I was in the desert or wilderness, starving—that's how I felt. The heavy doses of steroids, along with the destruction of my pituitary, resulted in me gaining close to 100 pounds. I went from being this taut, well-conditioned 145-pounder to this bloated 240-pounder. I had to get rid of all of my clothes. Nothing fit anymore. It really pained me to see this transformation because I had gotten myself into great shape in recent years. Not only had I become sober, but I had started working out daily with a fitness trainer who accompanied us on tour and doubled as a body guard. By working out religiously and altering my diet, I was in better shape in my forties than I had been in my twenties. But eradicating the tumor had changed all that—dramatically.

Five months after the surgery, I was married in a chapel in the woods along Keuka Lake, south of Rochester. The reception was held at a nearby Civil War–era mansion. I can remember the wedding ceremony. But when I looked at the pictures just a few weeks later, I wondered, "Who's that guy with my bride?" I had a difficult time recognizing myself, that's how much of a toll the operation and recovery had taken on me.

After I began getting back on my feet following the radiation treatments, I received a call from Mick. He inquired how I was doing, then he reminded me that Foreigner was committed to a rescheduled domestic and international tour in 1998 and '99. I told him I would do my best to be ready to go by then and asked him if we could postpone it for a while if I wasn't. He said we had signed iron-clad contracts before I was even diagnosed and there would be threats of lawsuits if we didn't follow through. Mick also laid an additional guilt trip on me. He said the band was counting on me—that this was our livelihood and some of the guys hadn't been wise with their finances and were in dire need of these paydays.

When it came time to hit the road for a few concerts in the summer of 1998, Dr. Black cleared me medically but said I needed to be very careful and warned me that I was still a long way from being back to my old self, both physically and mentally. Not that I needed any reminder. I noticed it every time I went to shave and saw this unrecognizable man staring back at me from the mirror. Although the swelling had gone down considerably, my face was still puffy from the steroids I had to take; there was no definition. I looked like Charlie Brown. It made me quite reluctant to go out in public because whenever I ran into somebody I knew, they wouldn't be able to hide their shock. They'd have these looks on their faces, like, "Oh my god, what happened to you, Lou?"

Despite all these issues, I decided to give it the old college try because I felt an obligation to the guys in the band. But in retrospect, it was an asinine decision that wound up hurting both me and Foreigner. I used to be a whirling dervish on stage—I was all over the place. But my weight gain, coupled with some serious balance issues caused by the swelling, forced me to plant myself like a statue in one place the entire concert. I became an immovable object, just like a drum set or the speakers. My greatest concern was with my memory. It still hadn't come back all the way, so there would be times when I would reach a certain point in a song and my mind would go blank. The scary and frustrating thing about that was these were lyrics I had helped write and had sung thousands of times before. It got so that I would write down certain lyrics in big letters on pieces of cardboard and place them at my feet during concerts. They were my security blanket.

The tour lasted several weeks with a few brief breaks thrown in here and there so I could return home for a few days. I was whipped all the time, and after the show, my head would be throbbing from the volume of our music. I was still taking about 10 to 12 pills a day for the various issues I was dealing with. I also had to inject myself daily with testosterone and another drug to fill the functions of my destroyed pituitary gland. Not surprisingly, I was not at the top of my game; far from it. My voice clearly wasn't back to full force. The problem was I couldn't get enough air into my diaphragm to sing the way I was used to singing. I had to breathe almost twice as hard, so in an attempt to rectify the problem, I started taking oxygen during shows. I'd wait for a drum or a guitar solo and head off to the side of the stage where the audience couldn't see me and put on the oxygen mask for about 30 seconds. It helped me get through the performances. Not having my full voice was like a pitcher not having his fastball. I had to improvise at certain points and sing around something instead of trying to nail it. I learned how to pace myself and save it for those moments when I really needed to hit some high notes. I made sure I took a hit of oxygen to get recharged before we played that string of really challenging songs like "Urgent" and "Juke Box Hero" near the end of the show. It definitely helped me avoid making a fool of myself.

I had to compensate wherever I could, and I hated doing that because I felt like I was compromising the integrity of the song, but I had no choice. And that just added to the misery and the guilt I was feeling because as the front man for our band, I always took great pride in giving our fans their money's worth.

But that wasn't possible given the condition I was in. I had to accept the fact that I needed to grind my way through.

Although what I had endured was public knowledge—we worked hard to get the word out to the media at every stop on tour—the critics were extremely cruel. Several of them tore me and the band to shreds. I actually heard some of the critics and concert-goers say things like, "Lou, you better back off those cheeseburgers and the pasta." I suppose I could understand some of the venom from people in the audience who might not have known the score. But there was no excuse for the personal attacks from the music critics because our publicist went out of his way to apprise rock journalists of my situation. I had read reviews since the band's formation two decades earlier, and I obviously didn't always care for the treatment we received, particularly the allegations that we were a corporate rock band that cared only about commercial success. But these reviews were far more brutal than anything we had ever received and went beyond the bounds of fair criticism in my mind. I tried to explain my story during the radio and newspaper interviews we did before each tour stop, but some people apparently didn't want to let the facts get in the way of what they thought was a good torch-job story. After a while, I stopped reading the papers and stopped listening to the radio stations in towns where we were performing.

As you can imagine, my health problems and the pressures of the tour put my faith and sobriety to a severe test. There were times, especially after shows, when I was so tempted to drown my sorrows in booze or drugs. And I wouldn't have had to go far to find the vices that once got me through the endless nights; they were all around me, readily available.

To distract myself, I would pull out my Bible and read verses I felt were applicable to the challenges I was facing. And on the really bad nights, I'd get on the phone with my pastor back in Rochester and we would talk and pray deep into the night. Some of my most challenging times came after shows when we'd have to board our bus to head for our next stop. Several of these trips were 8 to 10 hours long, and the boys in the band would be partying heavily the entire way. I would hole myself up in my sleeping compartment. I vividly remember nights when I would be stuffing T-shirts against the seams at the bottom of the compartment's folding doors to prevent the marijuana fumes from seeping in. And I would pray for hours to God to give me the strength not to give in. Despite being on the brink of joining the guys in their merriment on several occasions, I never gave in, never fell off the wagon. Although I've been sober for two decades and counting, I fully realize it is something I can never become cocky about. As I said before, I understand this is a day-to-day, hour-to-hour, minute-to-minute struggle that I must deal with for the rest of my life.

Not surprisingly, in the months following my surgery, I became depressed to the point where I needed help. I was real straight with my doctors, and they understood. They prescribed mild anti-depressants, just to take off that morose edge. That helped quite a bit. During this harrowing time, they also taught me to adjust my focus from the things I couldn't do and the hell I'd been through to the progress I was making. They reminded me that this was going to be a long slog but that I was improving and would continue to get better and would be able to live a good life again.

In retrospect, my fans—most of whom were total strangers to me—also helped me deal with the mental, physical, and emotional challenges I was facing during that vulnerable time. The letters and cards I received from them were incredibly uplifting. People would send me crosses and good-luck charms. Some would tell me that they had been through what I had been through. I even received a couple of letters from people who had been diagnosed with the exact same tumor, and I referred them to Dr. Black and Brigham & Women's Hospital. That I was able to help them out made me feel tremendous and reminded me of why God had given me this challenge.

From May through August 1999, we teamed with our arena-rock rivals, Journey, on a 55-city tour of North America. Some billed it as the Comeback Tour, because Journey was hitting the road with a new lead vocalist—Steve Augeri in place of Steve Perry—and we were doing our first extensive tour since my surgery, so people wanted to see if I still had it.

To conserve energy, I left the lion's share of the pre-concert publicity to Mick. I must admit, he was kind to me in his interviews with the press. In one story, he told the reporter, "It's a bloody miracle Lou's even out here. I look across the stage some nights because he's singing his ass off and tears come into my eyes, and I think, *Wow, this is life, this is the good part.* He's back on stage and it's absolutely amazing, and I think he's going to become a speaker for a foundation for brain-tumor patients because it's a wonderful story for people to gain confidence and support and say, 'Look at what this guy did.' It certainly puts things into perspective." It was one of the kindest things he had ever said about me.

For the most part, the tour was well received by longtime fans of the bands. But it didn't seem to have quite the energy of the early Foreigner tours. I'd be the first to admit that my condition certainly contributed to that, but again, what was I supposed to do in that situation? The bottom line is that I should not have been out touring. I should have been home recuperating and rehabbing to get my health back. But I believe there was another reason the tour underachieved. We had not produced a new album in more than three years, and although our fans loved the stuff from our glory years, I think they were also looking for some new hits from us.

After the tour ended, Mick wanted to get right to work on a new album, and that was unusual for him because normally he disappeared for months after we stopped performing. And to be honest, I could have used a hiatus at that point. Mick rented a beautiful mansion out in the Hamptons on Long Island and invited me there to start working with him on some new material. I was still having occasional problems putting my thoughts into words—there was still some lag time between thinking and verbalizing—and my doctors told me it would take time before this problem took care of itself. This obviously put a wrench in the creative process, and I could sense Mick's frustration with this plodding give-and-take. We'd do this for a few days, then I'd go back to Rochester, and we'd try to hook up again the following week, and it remained a struggle. By about our third or fourth unproductive session, Mick brought aboard this guy named Marty, who had done some work for Aerosmith, KISS, and Jon Bon Jovi. Next thing I know, the two of them are collaborating on songs I wasn't well enough to help create. I was just there to sing what they came up with.

I know Mick was gung-ho to produce a new album, and I understood why to a certain extent. But to bring this guy aboard to take over my role felt like an act of betrayal. My ego was crushed. Here I had just busted my ass touring when I shouldn't have been so the band would make money, and this was Mick's way of thanking me. The thing is that Mick and I had already written about six or seven songs for a new album. As it turned out, the collaboration between Mick and this hired gun never amounted to much. The album was never finished, and the songs he and I had worked on are still out there as far I know.

• • •

I truly believe in divine intervention. There's no doubt in my mind that God was looking after me during my ordeal with the brain tumor, and he sent some guardian angels to my rescue again about a year or two after my surgery. That's when I dozed off at the wheel on three separate occasions, resulting in two head-on collisions that nearly killed me and several others, including my twins. The first accident occurred on a winter's afternoon when I was driving back from a doctor's appointment in my '99 Chevy half-ton truck. I zonked out on a wooded road about two miles from my suburban Rochester home and crossed into the other lane—thank God no one was driving there at the time—and into the brush. I was jolted awake and tried to wrest control of my vehicle as I plowed through a row of saplings. I then crossed back over both lanes of the road before lurching to a stop after crashing into a stump near a ditch. I shook uncontrollably for about 10 minutes before unfastening my seat belt and climbing out of my truck. I was shocked when I surveyed the scene and saw the looping path I had taken. I examined my truck and noticed deep scratches on the fenders and hood. Both side mirrors had been torn off. One of my front tires had gone flat from the impact. I had the presence of mind to call a friend of mine who had an auto repair business, and he came with a flat-bed truck and brought it back to his shop.

Several months later, I was driving that same truck when I fell asleep and crossed into the other lane again. This time I was on a busy street, and I smashed head-on into an oncoming car. Miraculously, no one was hurt. After regaining consciousness,

I immediately checked on my twins, who were strapped into baby carriers in the back seat. They were crying and had a couple of bumps and bruises but were okay. The four people in the compact car I had collided with were taken to the hospital but were released immediately after being examined. I went back to my doctor and asked him if perhaps some of the medication I was on was causing these black-outs. But he insisted that couldn't be the case, that there had to be another cause.

Well, not long after that second accident, it happened again. I'm blinking and blinking and blinking, trying my best to stay awake while driving home in the late afternoon, but I fell asleep again. I drifted into the other lane and collided head-on with a car that had just pulled out of a side street. Thank God the woman in the totaled vehicle was okay. The next day I had a friend drive me to the motor vehicle department, and I turned in my license. I just couldn't trust myself behind the wheel any more.

I then went to my doctor to see if we could get to the bottom of my fatigue problems once and for all and he suggested that I go to a sleep disorder clinic for tests. They wired me up and monitored my sleeping patterns for an entire night. The tests showed emphatically that I was suffering from a severe case of sleep apnea. They determined that during the six hours I slept, I was getting less than 20 minutes of REM sleep. Throughout the night, I was constantly waking up, desperately gasping for air like a man with a noose around his neck. No wonder I had been falling asleep at the wheel and at various other times during the day. It was a tremendous relief to finally discover the cause of my fatigue and find a solution. My doctor put me on a CPAP machine to help me breathe freely at night, and it wasn't long before I began feeling like a human rather than a zombie again.

• • •

I had remarried about four months after my surgery, and in 1999 my second wife gave birth to our twins—Natalie and Joe. I was thankful to become a father again, and I vowed to myself that I was going to be a big part of their lives, that I wasn't going to short-change them the way I felt I had short-changed Nick and Matt, my sons from my first marriage. That's still one of the great regrets of my life. My career ambitions and some really bad lifestyle choices had deprived them of a full-time dad, and that's my fault. I can never get that time back with them, but I've tried my best to make amends and show them that I'm remorseful and that I love them.

Achieving true sobriety goes beyond abstinence. It's also about healing your soul, apologizing for damage you did to others, and seeking forgiveness. When I was at Hazelden Treatment Center, I realized that at some point I needed to have a heart-to-heart with Nick and Matt. I waited until a few years after I got out of rehab because I wanted Matt to be old enough to fully understand. Needless to say, it was one of the most difficult talks I've ever had. The boys were in their early twenties at the time and were actually working as part of our road crew. One night after a show, we grabbed a bite to eat and went back to my hotel room. We watched some television and made some small talk and then I said I had something I needed to speak to them about. I told them what my dreams and ambitions had been growing up and how I was blessed enough to realize those dreams but that my life got out of control. I said my job took me away from them more than I ever imagined, and I acknowledged that even when I was home I was still kind of away from them because I was consumed with my career and my bad habits. I rambled on for quite some time, baring my soul completely. At the end, I told them how sorry I was for not being the father I should have been but that I always loved them and always would. They didn't say anything right away. I could see that they were lost in thought for a while. I started crying and they started crying, and I hugged them like I never had before. I really think that night helped clear the air, and we've had a much better relationship ever since.

I'm proud of the young men they've become. One is a sous chef and has his own restaurant, and the other is a computer whiz who's experimenting with a number of different products, including a revolutionary low-fat coffee creamer he hopes to market nationwide. Neither of them had musical ambitions, and that's fine with me.

The birth of my twins clearly was a life-changing moment for me. As I mentioned, I was determined that they would grow up with an involved father, one who would be there for school functions and Little League games, and that's what I've tried to do. Their arrival forced me to take a much deeper look at what I wanted out of life. It caused me to rearrange my priorities. For too long it had been about my career, about my ambitions and desires, about me. But I was determined to change that. I was going to start putting my family first, my band second. I knew this change of heart wasn't going to play well with Mick. In fact, I knew he was going to be royally ticked off. Frankly, I didn't give a damn because the magic between us—the magic that enabled us to churn out an incredible string of hits during that six-year stretch—had disappeared. You can't always make it feel like the first time the second time around. His decision to bring in a hired gun to finish an album, particularly after the sacrifices I had made for Foreigner following my brain tumor surgery and radiation treatments, cut me to the core and caused irreparable damage.

I had also grown tired of being around the alcohol and drug scene. I had worked extremely hard to get where I was, and I didn't want to jeopardize my sobriety. The band's party-animal mindset no longer appealed to me. We were all in our late forties and early fifties for goodness sake. It was time to get a grip and grow up.

In a four-year span from 1999–2003, we released six more anthology albums. And that stagnation really bothered me. We hadn't created anything new and exciting. We were merely rearranging our old furniture, but the room was still the same. In essence, we had become like so many groups from our era—a has-been band that was resting on its laurels. And I hated that because I still yearned to create, still yearned to reinvent myself.

• • •

In April 2002, after nearly three decades of talking about it, we finally got my old group, Black Sheep, together for a reunion concert back in Rochester. It did me good to see us finally pull this off and perform again with guitarist Don Mancuso, drummer Mike Bonafede, keyboardist Larry Crozier, and bassist Bruce Turgon, whom I had recruited a few years earlier to join Foreigner. The organizers did a fabulous job and made me feel great. Before we took the stage of a packed house at the Water Street Music Hall, local bands Catch 22, Stranger, and Boys Lie covered several of my hits through the years. And during breaks, the organizers showed Foreigner concert footage provided by VH1. It had been 27 years since we had disbanded following the accident that destroyed our equipment, but I had always kept a soft spot in my heart for Black Sheep, and I had always hoped we could be reunited, even if it was just for a few days. I still believe that we would have made it to the big time had we not caught that bad break.

It was an unforgettable night, and afterward I couldn't help but wax nostalgic. "The swagger that the music had, and the attitude that we carried around, on and off the stage, with us—I miss that," I told Jeff Spevak, the music critic of the *Rochester Democrat and Chronicle*. "It felt good all day long to be in Black Sheep. I'm so glad we finally did this. It's been something we've kind of felt needed to be fulfilled." The other—and most important—thing about that night was that we were able to raise several thousand dollars for the Bright Eyes Fund of the Golisano Children's Hospital, a Rochester program that supports kids with brain tumors. Obviously, it remains a cause of particular interest to me.

The reunion concert warmed my soul and provided me with a brief respite from my troubles. Not long after our performance, my divorce from my second wife became official. The surgery and the long, arduous rehabilitation had taken its toll on our relationship, but I'll always feel blessed because that marriage resulted in the birth of Joe and Natalie, two of the greatest things that ever happened to me.

10

An End and a Beginning

After the Black Sheep reunion, I returned to Foreigner strongly sensing that a divorce from the group I had been a member of for nearly a quarter of a century was looming. Mick's decision to bring in another songwriter marked the beginning of the end for me. I told him that he could have the guy sing those songs, too, because I wasn't singing anything I didn't have a part in creating. I wasn't going back to the old ways that had precipitated my first departure from the band. He was not pleased with me, and our relationship became as strained as it had been before—as cold as ice. We didn't argue. There wasn't any open hostility between us, but conversations became minimal and there wasn't any interaction between us on stage during a July-September tour that featured stops throughout the United States as well as Vancouver and Mexico City.

The final straw came during the Night of the Proms tour we did in the Netherlands toward the end of 2002. They had assembled an All-Star band in which they had invited several performers—including the Pointer Sisters, Michael McDonald, the guys from Simple Minds, Mick, and me. By this time, Mick had really been hitting the booze and drugs hard despite claims that he had been sober and was even running his own AA meetings. As a recovering alcohol and drug addict, and as someone who had worked intimately with the guy for half our lives, I could see otherwise. My suspicions that he had fallen off the wagon were confirmed when our assistant tour manager went to stock Mick's refrigerator with bottled water and discovered a gigantic bottle of vodka. We played in the Netherlands for about three weeks and it was embarrassing because Mick would be so juiced that he would be screwing up notes he had played a million times. And the sad thing was he was so far gone he didn't realize it, even though members of the orchestra and audience could. The worst moment occurred near the end of the final concert of the tour when we sang "Let It Be." We were standing next to the Pointer Sisters, and Mick grabbed Bonnie Pointer's ass just as she started singing her portion of the song. This kind of behavior—in front of 40,000 people—we were all mortified.

I had pretty much had it with his shenanigans. Afterward, I met with our manager and told him that unless Mick sobered up, I was out of there. I said it was pointless to continue with Foreigner because Mick was too drunk and stoned to create any new music and it was affecting his performances on stage. Our manager said he understood my frustrations and that he was just as frustrated as I was. He told me that Mick had been in and out of rehab a few times in the past year, but they had a new plan they thought would work. They were going to fly him directly from the Netherlands to the Betty Ford Center where he would spend a solid month working on becoming sober. Unfortunately, that never happened. Unbeknownst to our manager and Mick's wife, Mick changed his flight and went to England instead where he continued to party hard with friends.

After that happened, I made my departure official. I was done with Foreigner—this time for good.

I felt good about my decision, and I returned to Rochester looking forward to spending time with Joe and Natalie, who had just turned four. I was ready to move on with my life and my career. It felt good to be back home.

I had hoped 2003 would be a year to soothe my soul and recharge my spirit. Instead, it turned out to be a draining and tragic time for me and my family. Within a seven-month span, I lost both my mom and dad—she from a heart attack after being in a coma for a year following what was supposed to be simple surgery, and he from non-smoker's lung cancer. It was a devastating blow to me and my brothers.

While all of this was going on, I asked Bruce Turgon, a bandmate from Black Sheep and Foreigner who co-wrote some of my solo album songs, to help put together a band. He did, and we went on tour. Although we played in front of packed houses in smaller venues, I wound up losing nearly $500,000 on the venture because of demands that Bruce and some of the other band members made in mid-tour and because of a poor deal I signed with the attorney who had arranged the tour. The experience left a sour taste in my mouth, and I disbanded the band. I didn't know what I would do next. I thought about bagging things for a while. There had been some rumors that I would try to reunite with Mick, but there wasn't any truth to them. I had enough of him for a lifetime. I was so done with Foreigner.

On his deathbed, Dad reminded me that it had been his and Mom's dream to see their three boys in a band together. And that definitely influenced my decision when I formed a new band. I enlisted both of my brothers and also went back to my old friends, Don Mancuso and Andy Knoll—people I had played with locally and people I trusted. In 2004, we went on tour with the Lou Gramm Band. And after the first concert we played, I remember my brothers and me coming off the stage and huddling for a moment in a corner. We said a prayer and told Mom and Dad, "That one was for you. Hope you were looking down on the show."

• • •

For the longest time, I had toyed with this idea of producing a Christian rock album. The seed was actually planted way back in 1991 when I was in rehab at Hazelden and accepted Jesus Christ as my savior. Over the next dozen or so years I would occasionally come across Bible verses or inspirational phrases and write them down in those spiral notebooks where I kept my song ideas. A few years after I broke away from Foreigner for the final time, I told the guys in my new band that I had made a promise to myself that my next album would have a Christian flavor. So instead of singing about hot babes, we'd be singing about God's influence on us, especially in trying times.

My bandmates kind of threw these sideways glances at me and asked, "Are you sure you want to go in this direction?" I told them that I was, and once I started writing the songs and they heard the approach I was taking, they became a lot more comfortable. The bottom line is that we were still recording rock songs and we were still telling stories. My references to the Lord were subtle. My intent wasn't to do a Bible-thumping beat-you-over-the-head Christian album. But I did want to convey how God had helped me through some pretty difficult times and how He had become a driving force in my life. We began slipping a few of the Christian songs into our concerts along with our established stuff, and the reception was very positive. A lot of people weren't even aware that these songs were going to be part of a Christian album that we released in 2009.

Artists often encounter difficulties when they imbue their faith into their music. There are concerns about how they will be received and perceived by the mainstream public. I know some people were gung-ho about me doing this. They understood what I had been through with my addiction problems and my brain tumor, and they thought it was really cool that I would write about how my faith pulled me through some harrowing times. And there were others who were shaking their heads and saying, "He really does have brain damage. He's gone."

I anticipated the prejudice I would face when people would say, "Enough of the God stuff." But the majority of listeners enjoyed the rock sound and the lyrics, too. Believers and non-believers alike were able to glean something from the music, and that was my intent. I was still a rock 'n' roll artist. It was still music that was fun to listen to and sing along with. It just had lyrics and a message that went deeper than most rock songs.

One of the toughest things for me was reconciling the sexual nature of my old songs with the more thoughtful tone of the new stuff. At one moment I'm belting out "Hot Blooded" or "Feels Like the First Time," and then I'm singing about religious faith. Boy meets girl vs. boy meets God certainly makes for a difficult, yet interesting contrast of ideas that are diametrically opposed. You can get attacked from both sides—the hard-line believers who feel you should stop playing what they perceive as the raunchy songs from the past, and those who don't want to feel as if they are being proselytized. I think we were able to do that high-wire act fairly well, and the majority of our fans accepted the past and the present.

I've been blessed through the years to have great fans—people who have followed me from the time I was an unknown with Black Sheep and have stuck with me through thick and thin. The interesting thing about my time with Foreigner is that we developed a strong following internationally, especially in Japan, where we toured several times. There was this one librarian from Tokyo who was so smitten with my performances that she would find out our schedule and time her vacation around our tours, often coming to the United States to see me play in those years when we didn't do the international gigs. She might qualify as my most loyal fan of all time. And fortunately, it's become a lot easier for her to catch me and my band in concert because she moved to New York City about 10 years ago. To reward her for her support, we send her an all-access pass each year that permits her to come backstage after the shows. I can't thank her enough for her dedication. It's been pretty remarkable.

And there are others like her, though maybe not on her level of loyalty. I like it when I'm out touring different parts of the country and I run into couples who remember coming to a Foreigner concert when they were teenagers and are now coming to concerts as parents and grandparents. And I'm surprised at how many of them tell me that they've seen us play four or five times during this tour. Of course, when they start showing you pictures of their grandchildren, it makes you feel really old.

There is another side to fandom that can be scary. There are some crazy people out there—people who attempt to stalk you, and that's really uncomfortable. We've actually had situations where we've had to alert security and the local police about death threats and get orders of protection banning certain individuals from concerts. I remember one time after Foreigner's first album came out. I was in my hotel room after a performance, and I heard this guy pounding and screaming on Mick's door. The guy was either drunk or strung out or both, and he was screaming that Mick had stolen one of his songs and he was going to make him pay. We called security.

Most of the time, it's either deranged people or individuals who are inebriated or stoned. But you have to take these things seriously. It's a side of celebrity that people don't think about, but it exists. By the mid-1980s, I actually hired my trainer to travel with me on the road to double as my body guard. It served two purposes to have him with us—he helped keep us in peak physical condition by running us through his regimen of conditioning programs, and his black-belt training and background as a kick-boxer helped keep any crazies from getting too close to us.

Concerts can lead to some interesting behavior by fans, particularly those who are liquored- or coked-up and feeling no pain. Through the years, I've had women throw panties, bras, hotel room keys, and wadded up pieces of paper with their phone numbers onto the stage. There were times when we'd be boarding our bus following a concert and half-naked women would break through the security line and throw themselves at you, telling you that they wanted to ride the bus with us to the next city. I'm happy to report that stuff doesn't happen to me anymore. I still will have "gifts" tossed on the stage, but now they're usually framed Bible verses, crosses, and inspirational poems.

Every concert venue is different in size and configuration, and you want to make sure that you avoid situations where crowds can get too unruly and people might get hurt. We've played places where we've actually had people thrown on to the stage by security people to help them avoid being crushed. And we've played places where a number of fights break out and you have to stop the music until order is restored. Believe me, we're always apprised in advance of where the backstage exits are and how many security people will be in place, just in case. Fortunately, I've never experienced a riot or a tragedy in the thousands of concerts I've played, but I've seen some bad stuff going on in the crowds and it can be a little unsettling. It doesn't take much for a few rowdies to turn a concert into a riot and a tragedy, so you have to be aware.

Perhaps the strangest concert I've ever been involved in was in Union City, Michigan, in August 1995. That was the first and only time we ever performed at a nudist colony. And you might say we were caught with our pants down—metaphorically, of course—because we had no idea that we, along with Kansas and Blue Oyster Cult, would be performing in front of bare-naked ladies and men until our bus arrived at the venue. As we got closer to the place, we began noticing these "Nudestock" signs. That prompted a couple of us to get out of our seats and ask, "What the hell is going on here? What is this place?" By then Mick's brother, Kevin Jones, who was our tour manager, was laughing so hard he was crying. He said, "Didn't you guys know? This is a nudist colony you are performing at." We thought for sure he was pulling our leg. But as we got closer to the stage, we realized he wasn't kidding. "I'm not going out there," I said. And my bandmates began echoing my protests. Kevin told us that we had no choice but to play because we were contractually obligated. "The show must go on," he said, still laughing hard.

So the show did go on, and it was quite bizarre. Usually when I sing, I like to make eye contact with different segments of the audience as I move around the stage. But that evening, I found myself spending a lot of time looking up at the sky or down at my feet. I just couldn't bear—pardon the pun—to look at the audience. The funny part was that most of the people at the concert were in their fifties and sixties, so when they were dancing, the women's boobs were bumping against their knees and the guys' stomachs were bouncing around like a bunch of beach balls. Let's just say it was not a pretty sight.

• • •

I've always tried to accommodate autograph seekers. In the old days, it was actually easier because you knew people were collecting them for themselves or a relative or a friend. But nowadays, with the explosion of eBay, you'll have professional autograph hounds show up with 15 albums they want signed. You ask, "Who would you like this made out to?" and they'd say, "Oh, just put your name on it." They don't want it personalized because that will drive the value way down. Again, I'm a willing signer, but I have no use for the professional autograph dealers trying to make a buck off my name.

We always had a strong following overseas, and we loved playing in Europe, Japan, and Australia. Some foreign audiences are similar to American audiences. We were huge in Germany, and they were every bit as rowdy as U.S. concert-goers. We would be playing in Berlin or Munich and the fans would be singing along in English and sometimes German. The crowds in Japan were much more subdued but every bit as appreciative in their own way. I remember doing concerts in Tokyo at 5:00 in the afternoon, and you'd look out from the stage and see all these Japanese students in their school uniforms. We'd be belting out our tunes, feeling like we were at the top of our game, and when we finished our songs, there would be a pause and then polite applause. They were just as passionate about us and our music, but culturally they were more subdued and polite, so their response wasn't nearly as raucous as concert-goers here and in Europe. But we knew how much they were into us because our record sales in Japan were always enormous.

• • •

After I got divorced for a second time in 2003, I was certain I would never marry again. I felt there might come a time when I dated again, but marriage was out of the question; it was just never going to happen. Thanks to Robyn Butera, I learned to never say never. And thanks to her I learned how to love again and decided to give marriage a third try. I was introduced to Robyn about six or seven years ago at Abbott's, a Rochester ice cream chain famous for its scrumptious frozen custard. But I didn't really begin to get to know her until a few years later when she and her cousin started showing up at a weekly car cruise I went to in one of the city's suburbs.

One night after I pulled in, Robyn's cousin came up to me and started talking and wouldn't stop. I couldn't help but look a few steps beyond her because there stood Robyn, who said "Hi" to me and little else. After listening to her cousin chew my ear off for about 20 minutes, I politely excused myself, telling her I needed to check out the cars before people began leaving. The next week, I showed up and Robyn and her cousin were there, and the same thing happened. The cousin did all the talking; Robyn didn't say boo. And on the rare occasions that I tried to strike up a conversation with Robyn, the cousin would cut her off.

Unbeknownst to me, she had told Robyn she was going to put the moves on me and that Robyn should steer clear. After about the third week of this, her cousin finally got around to asking me if I would like to go out for a date. I told her that was very nice of her but that I would rather just remain friends. Well, she didn't like that response at all and stomped off. I grinned at Robyn and she grinned sheepishly at me before following after her cousin.

I went back to that same car cruise the next couple of weeks in hopes that Robyn would be there, but she wasn't. Finally, after about two or three weeks, she did show up again with her brother and without her cousin. Robyn and I hit it off immediately. We had a lot of fun and a lot of laughs as we moseyed from car to car. She got to meet my twins at a few of the cruises, and I could see them bonding with her. There was an upcoming fundraiser for a person battling cancer and I asked her if she would like to join me and the twins. That was our first date, and we were off and running from there. I obviously was initially attracted to her because she is a gorgeous woman. And the more time I spent with her, I began to see that her beauty went way beyond her looks. I found her to be a woman of great depth and compassion. I learned about how her mom had died young and how Robyn quickly assumed the role of family caregiver—a role she continues to assume today while looking after her dad who has to undergo weekly kidney dialysis treatments.

Although I believed I would never become attached to anyone again, I couldn't help myself and neither could she. We fell in love, and in August 2010 I popped the question. We were married the following June in suburban Rochester, and

I couldn't be happier. The third time in my case has definitely been a charm.

• • •

My fascination with cars traces to my early youth. I have fond memories of riding in my dad's car—a 1953 Pontiac that he had bought used a year or two later. I loved the look of that vehicle, and before you knew it, I was admiring and learning about the other types of cars in our neighborhood and beyond. There were a couple of teenagers on our street with their own cars, and I remember how they had taken off the hub caps and painted the rims red. That was their rebellious way of making their cars distinctive and sportier. I thought it was very cool and vowed to myself that I would do something similar when I got my first car.

When I was eight years old, I was riding with my uncle and aunt when my uncle started talking about how much he liked such-and-such a car. I told him that he had gotten the make and model of the car mixed up, that it really was a such-and-such. And he said, "Oh, you think you know your cars, huh? Well, what kind of car is that over there?" I immediately reeled off the make and model. "What about that one?" he asked, pointing at another vehicle. I answered correctly again. "And that one? And that one over there?" He finally said, "Louie, I guess you really do know your cars."

A few years later, I spent a couple of days in the hospital with rheumatic fever. My dad brought me a get-well gift—a small-scale, metal model of a 1960 Chrysler New Yorker. It was painted in two-tone green, and I marveled at the detail. I had already been putting together model airplanes and boats, but after I was released from the hospital I started a new hobby—putting together model cars. As I assembled and glued together those models, I dreamed about the day I'd be able to afford a real car.

That dream materialized when I was about 16 years old. I had saved up about $800 working after school and on weekends at Valenti's Furniture Store. For some time, I had my eye on this 1956 Chevy two-door hardtop at this used-car dealership and when I finally accumulated enough money I hightailed it over there and bought the vehicle. I was so ecstatic you would have thought I had just won the lottery. The guy who sold me the car let me borrow some dealer plates so I could drive it off the lot. I felt like the coolest cat in town as I roared down my street and into our driveway. I revved the engine a few times, and my dad and mom came out to see what was making all this noise. I noticed right away that Pops wasn't wearing the same excited look I was.

"Louis, what did you do?" he said, and I immediately realized I was in trouble because he was calling me "Louis."

"I bought this car, Dad," I responded. "Isn't she a beauty?"

"Louis, I'm disappointed you didn't even talk to me about this," he said.

"I'm sorry, Dad, but I've been eyeing this car for some time. I think it's a great car."

"Oh, you do? Get out of the car, and we'll see how great it is."

I did as he said, and he began his inspection. It took all of a few seconds for him to show me that this car wasn't as great as I thought it was. Dad peeled back the rubber floor mat on the driver's side, and you could see through to the driveway; the floor panel was rusted out. He then started the engine and clouds of black smoke shot out of the exhaust pipes. The car had been blowing smoke all the way from the dealer's lot, but I was too excited to notice.

Dad told me that we were going back to that dealer and getting our money back, and that's what we did. He drove my car, and I went with my mother in our family car. When we got there, my dad stormed into the dealer's office and threw the plates on the counter. "I want my money back now!" my father shouted at the dealer. "You sold this car to a minor, and you tried to take advantage of him. Either you give me my money back now, or I'll press charges against you so fast your head will spin." The guy didn't say anything. He gave me dirty looks, then went to his cash box and pulled out the money. When he finished counting out $800, my father grabbed the money, threw the keys on the counter, and stomped out.

"Louis, I hope you've learned a lesson," my father said, as we began driving home.

I had. The next time I purchased a car, Dad came with me.

My big brother, Ben, was also into cars—and mischief. My dad had this beautiful '63 Buick LeSabre with a powerful Wildcat engine. It was his pride and joy. When Ben and I were teenagers we would wait for Dad to pack it in for the night and we would put the LeSabre into neutral and push it out of the driveway and down the street a few houses before turning on the ignition key. We'd go cruising around town in this big tank, sometimes not getting back home until midnight. We'd always make sure we put gas back into the car and parked it exactly where we had found it in the driveway. Amazingly, we never got caught, but we came close a time or two because Dad was a stickler about his gas gauge, and he knew exactly what it read each time he parked that car in our driveway. A few times we put in more gas than we had used and he got a little suspicious, but he never found out about our shenanigans.

I loved muscle cars in particular. I loved the way they looked, the way they sounded, the way they accelerated. You couldn't have enough horse power as far as I was concerned. The roar of one of these thunderous engines remains music to my ears, still stirs my soul. My infatuation with speed really took off when I was about 16 or 17 and began hanging around with my band's bass player. Butch was about 10 years older than me, and he drove this black '65 GTO with red interior that made him very cool in my eyes. He often picked me up for rehearsals and shows, and after we finished playing, he would drive me to this dive of a restaurant in a run-down area of Rochester where all the greasers hung out.

Not long after I met him, he traded in that GTO for a black-on-black 1967 Dodge Charger with an even more powerful engine. And it was in that car that I experienced the adrenaline rush of my first drag races. Illegal drag races, I should add. Two cars would head from that restaurant parking lot onto the street and line up at a traffic light. They'd rev their engines and when the light switched to green, the drivers would floor their accelerators and race side-by-side down these city streets. The primary strip wound up being Lake Avenue, and the cars sometimes would hit 90 mph. You'd go pedal-to-the-metal for about a quarter of a mile before cooling it. And then the next two cars behind you would line up for their sprint. Everybody would eventually wind up at the Lake Ontario beach area in Charlotte. There they'd chill a bit, grab an ice cream, talk about their cars, then line up to race down Lake Avenue in the other direction. These sprints became a ritual on Friday and Saturday nights in the summer—a ritual, of course, not publicized by the Rochester Chamber of Commerce.

I was just a passenger in these sprints at first, and I was hooked by the sensation of speed and the element of danger. When I bought my third car—a '66 Olds 442 with a dark green exterior and black vinyl top—I was ready to become a racer rather than a passenger. I kept that car for a little while before selling it to my brother and buying a silver-and-black 1969 Chevy Nova with a turbo racing transmission and black interior. That car was an absolute animal, and it enabled me to win many a race up and down Lake Avenue.

As I mentioned, these street races were illegal and highly dangerous. I hate to admit it, but that was part of the allure. By 1971 or '72, the Lake Avenue drag races became a thing of the past as people living along the route began calling the police and patrol cars replaced the muscle cars that roared up and down this boulevard.

Many songs are obviously autobiographical, and my racing experiences wound up inspiring "Rev on the Red Line," which appeared on Foreigner's *Head Games* album in 1979. Al Greenwood, our keyboardist, had the musical idea, and I wrote the lyrics. A car's tachometer measures how fast your engine revs and it includes a red line. If you rev your car past this red line, you can blow your engine. And that happened on occasion during these sprints up and down Lake Avenue. Being an American, Al was familiar with a young man's obsession with fast cars and these unofficial drag races that took place throughout the states back in the day. But the Brits in the band didn't get this paean to fast cars and lawlessness and thought the song would flop. Fortunately, we were able to convince them otherwise, and it became one of our most requested concert songs, especially in the south and west, where it became a cult hit.

Two in a row, everybody knows
At the green light you rev it on the red line
Been waitin' all week to get my wheels on the street
Get my hands on the wheel, slide down in the seat

She's wearin' new colors and runnin' pretty good
I got four hundred horses tucked under the hood
But there's no need to panic, it's under control
We're aerodynamic and ready to roll

Rev on the red line
You're on your own
Rev on the red line
Just let it go

A lot of entertainers and athletes have been obsessed with fast cars, and some have turned their hobbies into second careers. One of the most successful, of course, was Paul Newman, who wound up racing at tracks around the country and acquitted himself quite well. After earning some big bucks from our early albums with Foreigner, I began toying with the idea of becoming a drag racer on the side. I went so far as to talk to some people in the industry and crunch some numbers, but I never followed through with it because it was going to force me to invest too much time, and the last thing I wanted was to spend even more time on the road away from my family. I did compete—legally this time—in a few drag races at Spencer Speedway and New York International near Rochester in the mid-1990s. I had just purchased this beautiful 1967 Chevy Chevelle Super Sport deluxe two-door sedan, and it had a racing history; it actually came with some old *Hot Rod* magazines that featured some stories about it. The car cost me $27,000, which is still the most I've spent on a muscle car. I raced about a dozen times, and although I didn't win any trophies, I more than held my own, winning several races along the way.

Classic muscle cars are my main hobby. (You might even call them my obsession.) At one point, I owned as many as nine, but I've since pared back my collection a bit. I try to find cars that were extremely well cared for by their original owners. That way I just have to fix the little things—like setting them up with some rally wheels and big tires. In addition to that Chevelle, I have a '65 Olds 442 with 47,000 original miles on it, a '68 Camaro 396/375 Super Sport black-on-black with 18,000 original miles, and a 1987 Buick Turbo-T that I bought brand new. They're my pride and joy, and I love driving them to cruise nights in the summer so I can see the wide variety of classic cars out there and what people have done to them. The cruises are great social events, almost like tailgating parties that you see before football games. As I learned during my courtship of Robyn, you meet a lot of interesting people at cruises. I enjoy leafing through classic car magazines and checking out classic car websites and swap meets. I'm often in search of parts, etc. The problem with classic cars is that it isn't easy replacing things on them because they don't make these vehicles any more, and in many cases they haven't for decades. So you sometimes have to go on a wild goose chase to find what you need. And there are cases when you come up blank and have to have a machinist make the part from scratch for you.

One last car story. After I released my second solo album, we performed on *The Tonight Show* with Jay Leno, and in between playing "Midnight Blue" and "Just Between You and Me," Jay called me over to sit down and talk. We chatted about our new album, and then I said, "Hey Jay, I heard you are a muscle car guy." He looked at the audience and dead-panned, "Where did you hear that?" Everybody burst out laughing. I told him I had a few cars, too. But I was a pauper compared to him. He has warehouses filled with cars and people on staff to maintain them. We were like two big kids discussing toys. We could have talked cars all night. That's how crazy we are about our hobby.

EPILOGUE

I frequently get asked about Foreigner's omission from the Rock 'n' Roll Hall of Fame. I think, given our body of work, we belong. And there apparently are thousands of music fans—and even many critics—who agree.

There have been online petition drives and Facebook pages devoted to the cause. Phil Marder, from *Goldmine: The Music Collectors Magazine,* wrote a column a few years ago that advocated our induction and kind of summed up people's views. The piece was cleverly titled: "It's Urgent—get Foreigner into the Rock Hall of Fame." Phil talked about how we had provided many outstanding moments between 1977 and 1988 in "a hit-filled career that should spell Hall of Fame inductee... why Foreigner has been ignored thus far is a mystery. After all, they are one of the biggest selling bands of The Rock era and they did it on Atlantic Records, the label that already has placed almost its entire roster, deserving or not, into Rock's Hall. Foreigner has had No. 1 albums in five different countries—the United States, the United Kingdom, Germany, Norway, and Switzerland, and nine top 10 singles in the U.S. alone. The run began with 'Feels Like the First

Time,' which hit No. 4 for the six-piece band fronted by former Spooky Tooth guitarist Mick Jones of England and American Lou Gramm, who would prove to be not only a fine songwriting partner for Jones, but one of Rock's most versatile vocalists as well." Marder concluded, by writing: "Foreigner was a heavy band that happened to have hit singles. Foreigner was a heavy band that happened to have a couple huge-selling ballads. These successes should not be held against the group. A behemoth of the '70s and '80s music scene, Foreigner earned its spot in the Rock & Roll Hall of Fame."

Our stats certainly stack up well to the competition. We had one less top 10 single than The Eagles, the same number as Fleetwood Mac, and more upper echelon hits than AC/DC; Led Zeppelin; Journey; Crosby, Stills & Nash; ZZ Top; Alice Cooper; David Bowie; and Bob Dylan. By no means am I saying that we were better than any of those acts. I'm just saying that we had—and continue to have—a pretty massive fan base, too, and that we must have been doing something right musically to be that consistent and that enduring.

A website devoted to AOR (Adult Oriented Rock) recently listed its top 50 albums from the 1970s and 1980s, and included three from Foreigner and one of my solo albums (*Ready Or Not*). They ranked our 4 album number three from that era, and they also wrote that "Juke Box Hero," "Cold as Ice," "That Was Yesterday," and "Midnight Blue" were "must-hear" singles.

I have no idea how the voting for the Hall works, nor do I care. It would be a tremendous honor if it ever happened, but I don't lie awake at night worrying about it. I'm told that Mick was ticked off about our exclusion and actually met with the people in charge of the inductions. I guess it started off cordially, but devolved when Mick lost his temper. By the time he walked out of that meeting one of the officials told him it would be a cold day in hell before Foreigner gets in. Again, I think we belong, but I have much more important things in life with which to concern myself.

Besides, Mick and I can take pride that we're in arguably a more prestigious club—the Songwriters Hall of Fame. That organization, which was formed in 1969, says its mission is to "shine a spotlight on the accomplishments of songwriters who have provided us with the words and music that form the soundtrack of our lives." I was tickled pink when I found out we were going to be inducted in 2013 because it was another indication that many of our songs have stood the test of time. And that's something Mick and I strove for when we were creating our music. We wanted to make songs that lasted not only for years, but for decades.

The neat thing about the Songwriters Hall is that it recognizes all genres of popular music—not just rock. So in addition to rockers like Chuck Berry, Roy Orbison, Bruce Springsteen, Elton John, and, of course, Lennon and McCartney, you'll find people like Irving Berlin, Aretha Franklin, Bob Dylan, Henry Mancini, Carly Simon, Stevie Wonder, Leonard Bernstein, Merle Haggard, Dolly Parton, James Brown, and Francis Scott Key. (Yes, the man who wrote "The Star-Spangled Banner" is a member, too. In fact, one of the charter inductees.) It's quite an eclectic mix, and I'm thrilled the committee believed we were worthy of being included in such rarified company.

The other great thing about the induction is that it sparked a reconciliation between Mick and me. To be honest, there was a time when I wondered if our heretofore cold-as-ice relationship would ever thaw. I'm so happy it did. Not long after being contacted by the folks at the Songwriters Hall, I picked up

the phone and called Mick. I was nervous dialing his number
because it had been 12 years since we last spoke, and the wounds
were still raw. But the minute we began talking, my anxiety
disappeared. We congratulated each other and reminisced briefly
about the good times and how our songwriting chemistry had
created an enduring body of work. Yes, there had been a lot of
hurt between us, but it was time to bury the hatchet and focus
instead on the magical alliance we once had.

    That June, the Songwriters Hall of Fame held its big
induction gala at the Marriott Marquis's massive ballroom in New
York City. The organizers asked us to perform two of our hits—
"Juke Box Hero" and "I Want to Know What Love Is." The day
before the ceremony, I showed up for rehearsal with Mick and
the session players who would be backing us. It was the first time
I had seen Mick since our breakup, and, as you might imagine, it
was extremely emotional. We hugged and said how good it was to
see each other. It was like being reunited with a family member
you hadn't seen in ages. As we rehearsed, the years melted away.
Mick was strumming his guitar with all his might. I was singing
from my soul. It really did feel like the first time as we journeyed
back in time.

    The night of the ceremony, Billy Joel introduced us.
He said we were juke box heroes back when there were juke
boxes, and added that "our staple of rock 'n' roll hits had forged
a legacy that still resonated with generations of fans." We made
a few quick remarks, then it was time to do what we had done
tens of thousands of times before. The banquet-goers went
wild the instant they heard the first chords of "Juke Box Hero,"
immediately springing to their feet and singing and dancing along
with us as if they were in a concert hall rather than a ballroom. For
about five minutes, it was the late 1970s, early 1980s again, when

Mick and I were on top of the rock world. We had been blessed with many memorable performances in our careers, but that one, at the Songwriters Hall of Fame ceremony, may have been the most poignant.

With the wall between us torn down, fans began clamoring for a Foreigner reunion tour. Mick seemed gung-ho about this, and I was, too. He also seemed enthused about my suggestion that the two of us get back into the studio to finish a number of songs we had worked on as part of a new album we had planned to produce before our split in 2004. I had the demos, and the songs sounded really good. With some tweaking here and there, we could help them reach their true potential.

Regarding the live concerts, I believed a mini-tour with just the original band members was the way to go. Nothing too extravagant or taxing. After all, we are all in either our late sixties or early seventies, and Mick was just a few years removed from major heart surgery and had been dealing with some other health problems that had reduced his touring significantly. I figured we could do hour-long shows in select cities, or set up shop in Las Vegas and perform there for several weeks. There's no doubt in my mind such a tour would have been a rousing success, but Foreigner's managers had other ideas. After being kept in the dark for a long time, we finally got word that they wanted to mix the old and new Foreigner bands at select concerts to celebrate the 40th anniversary of the release of *Double Vision*. The idea was to have the current band play hits from different eras, and the original members would then come on stage to do several songs from the *Double Vision* album.

There was a certain validity to their decision. After all, the "new" band had been touring as Foreigner for the past 10 years. The fans that remembered me and the other originals were still large in number and true diehards, but many of them had stopped attending concerts. There also was a large number of young fans who never knew any Foreigner but the current edition. None of the original members were pleased about the arrangement, but we realized if we truly wanted to participate in any kind of reunion we'd have to swallow hard. And no one would have to swallow harder than me, because for 26 years I had been the voice and face of the band—the front man—and had co-written so many of the songs.

I never felt ill will toward Kelly Hansen, the singer Mick hired to replace me. He has a strong voice, and Mick has trained him to mimic my sound, note for note, fairly well. Kelly captures every lyrical and phonetic nuance that's on the records. But I'm only human, and the sad thing for me is that younger people come to the shows and they don't even think twice about who they are listening to. They don't know the band's history. They just embrace the music, unaware that Kelly's not the original lead vocalist. To me, that's false advertising and shows no respect for Foreigner's history, but, hey, what are you going to do? Band rosters change. Time marches on. It's up to music fans to decide.

The thing that may have ticked off me and some of the original band members the most was when Mick re-recorded our self-titled *Foreigner* album a few years ago, using Hansen and the current crew rather than re-mastering our originals. He also redid the original cover, subbing the current musicians. To me, that was going too far. It was a really low blow and an insult to the guys who made those hits.

Yes, all bands go through personnel changes, and Foreigner has gone through more people than most bands I know. Mick's health problems have precluded him from being at numerous concerts in recent years, meaning it's reached a point where Foreigner often now performs without a single original member. Which begs the question—are you really listening to Foreigner or a glorified cover band playing Foreigner's catalogue?

All that aside, I wanted to move on and heal old wounds. Although the reunion wasn't going to be structured as I had envisioned, with just the original band members, the important thing was to forgive and reunite. Mick and I had created enduring music and had performed it passionately in front of millions of people around the world through the decades, and it was time to celebrate that collaboration and put an end to our feud. So, when I was told the first reunion gig would be on July 21, 2017, at the Jones Beach Theater on Long Island, I checked my ego at the door.

Again, I had harbored no animosity toward Kelly. I didn't meet him for the first time until I showed up for sound check several hours before that first mixed reunion concert. I didn't know what to expect from that first meeting. I didn't know if he was going to be cocky; if he was going to treat me like some rock 'n' roll has-been, like yesterday's news. I'm happy to report that he was very respectful and very friendly the instant I met him, and that put me immediately at ease. He told me it had been an honor to sing the songs I had sung and written for Foreigner. He also said it was an even bigger honor to be sharing the stage with me and that if there was anything he could do, to please let him know. He was very classy and gracious, and I couldn't have been more pleased about how he defused what could have been an extremely awkward and uncomfortable situation.

Several of the guys from the original band—Mick, me, keyboardist Al Greenwood, and multi-instrumentalist Ian McDonald—rehearsed for about a week before that first concert, and those sessions were really cool. It was great reconnecting not only with Mick, but the other guys, too. I had kept in touch with a couple of the original band members through the years. Some had gone on to very interesting and fulfilling post-Foreigner lives. As I mentioned, Dennis Elliott gave up his music career many years ago to pursue his other love—woodworking. He's an extremely gifted carver and has won numerous artistic awards for his work. And Al became the head procurer at the Manhattan Museum of Art. I was so happy they were able to find other pursuits to sate their creative appetites.

I was a little anxious heading into those rehearsals before our first reunion concert. What if the guys were really rusty? Or, even worse, what if they couldn't play anymore? What if we took the stage and were absolutely atrocious? We'd be viewed sadly, like Willie Mays was at the end of his Hall of Fame baseball career, stumbling after a fly ball while playing out the string with the New York Mets. Fortunately, my fears were quickly allayed. I found out Al and Ian had rented a studio weeks earlier and went through each song we were going to perform to ensure that the tempo and rhythm were buttoned up. When we took the stage and started playing, I was kind of stunned by how sharp we sounded. That first reunion concert couldn't have gone better, as we played three songs: "Long, Long Way from Home," "I Want to Know What Love Is," and "Hot Blooded." I think the original band sounded like we had in our prime. The crowd couldn't have been more enthusiastic. It was just like old times. We had managed to turn back the clock. A special night all the way around.

In interviews and during the times we appeared at those handful of reunion concerts, Mick reiterated that he and I were going to collaborate on some unfinished songs. I was stoked about that, but that still hasn't happened and I'm afraid, given Mick's health problems, it's never going to happen. I hope I'm wrong, but it doesn't look good that those songs will ever see the light of day.

• • •

After leaving Foreigner for good in 2004, I formed the Lou Gramm Band, and we wound up touring nationally and internationally. I was blessed during those years to be backed by some really talented musicians, people such as guitarist Don Mancuso, bass player A.D. Zimmer, keyboardist Andy Knoll, guitarist Michael Staertow, keyboardist Jeff Jacobs, saxophonist Scott Gilman, drummer Rob Mount, and my brother, Ben Grammatico, who spent two tours of duty with us, on the drums. When I was putting the band together I made a conscious effort to have most of the guys based in Rochester. That way we could get together and rehearse at the drop of a hat. And Ben was only an hour's flight away in New York City. His grandson lives in Rochester, so rehearsals gave him a chance to reconnect.

Donnie and I had been friends and colleagues since the Black Sheep days. Like I said, I think his first show with us was on the night of his high school graduation. We had heard about him through friends of friends. We wound up auditioning quite a few guys and were almost at the point where we didn't think there was anybody that was going to work out. We were desperate and didn't know what we were going to do, and then Donnie started strumming his six-string for us and we knew we had found our guy. He originally was more of a blues guitar player and that fit Black Sheep well. Donnie played good and looked good on stage and he was very easy to get along with because he was so laid-back. But he wasn't laid back to the point of not thinking. He was a very creative guy. He wasn't just along for the ride. He was a guy I stayed in touch with after Black Sheep had met its unfortunate demise. Whenever I took a break from Foreigner and was back in town, I would go watch him play and hang out with him. And I thought so much of him as a musician that when I did break away from Foreigner and went solo I sought him to play on my albums.

My band also had a great bunch of roadies, led by crew chief Bob Golino, who did a little bit of everything for us— from booking trips to driving vans to repairing speakers and instruments to selling merchandise. Bobby was one of those glue-who-holds-everything-together-kind-of-guys. Without behind-the-scenes people like him, the shows don't go on.

In recent years, I started scaling things back to about 30– 35 concerts a year, playing gigs mostly on Fridays and Saturdays. You've heard of weekend warriors. Well, I became a weekend rocker. I had solid reasons for downshifting. Part of it had to do with concessions we all make to age. I can still hit the high notes, but I don't believe my voice—or any 69-year-old's voice, for that matter—is resilient enough to hold up under the demands of three, four, five concerts a week. Especially when you have to sing songs as demanding as ours. And I didn't want to give my fans a subpar performance just so I could rake in a few extra bucks. We tried to structure our sets so there were enough up-tempo and mid-tempo songs, and we occasionally threw in a ballad. I think we provided a pretty entertaining mix of my solo material, my Foreigner classics, and an occasional newer tune.

As I indicated, my family also played a role in me wanting to cut back on my tour schedule. I didn't want to miss out on my twin's lives or the life of our newest member—daughter Luciana, whom Robyn gave birth to in 2017. I've made every attempt to be there for them as much as possible, and I knew I couldn't have done that if I attempted to tour like some driven twenty- or thirty-something rocker. Both of my twins—Joe and Natalie—were gifted musicians. Occasionally, they'd come to concerts and I'd bring them up on stage to sing backup on a song or two. They got a kick out of that and the audience seemed to, also. Neither Joe nor Natalie wanted to pursue a career in music, and I'm somewhat thankful for that because I've seen the high peaks and the deep valleys of this business. But if it had been their dream career, I would have supported them wholeheartedly. Joe and Natalie currently are attending my alma mater—Monroe Community College—and working at Wegmans, the nationally renowned, trend-setting grocery store chain headquartered in Rochester. Joe has been working in one of the store's pharmacies and has become so interested in the field that he might pursue a career as a pharmacist. Natalie hasn't decided what she wants to do with her life, and that's okay. She has plenty of time to figure things out.

• • •

A few years ago, I began giving serious thought to disbanding my band. It had nothing to do with my guys. They were quality musicians, still at the top of their game, still playing their hearts out each time we took the stage. And I really appreciated that. I also felt I was still giving our concertgoers their money's worth, and I still enjoyed the reaction of the fans to our performances. But after spending most of my adult life on the road, I had grown weary of the travel. I've lost track of all the time I've spent in airplanes, buses, and hotel rooms. I know this is part of the deal when you choose this type of career, but I had reached the point where enough was enough. I had spent too much time away from the people I love. I think the older you get, the more vulnerable you become. The glory of performing no longer could make up for the hurt and loneliness brought about by the separation from loved ones. I needed to down-shift a bit.

Plus, the economics of running a band had become

much more difficult. It's one thing when you have a huge record contract, and all the expenses—band salaries, transportation, lodgings, promotion, insurance, etc.—are taken care of by Atlantic or Capitol Records. It's quite another thing when you are responsible for all that stuff on your own. There were times when it was a losing proposition for me. You'd look at the spread sheets and realized this didn't make sense—or cents.

In November 2018, after months of deliberation and about six weeks before the end of our tour, I informed the guys that I was going to retire the band after the final concert that year. It was tough news to break, but I think they understood where I was coming from. I reiterated that this wasn't about them; that they were still playing their tails off. I thanked them profusely and told them how much I enjoyed them being a part of the band and how we had really played some terrific shows together.

The timing felt right to me. I experienced a tremendous sense of relief after I made the decision. I equate it to a ballplayer who can still hit and field, but had lost a certain something, and doesn't want to continue on anymore without that certain something. Sure, they could play a few more years, but the game's not the same for them, not as easy or natural to them as it once was. I didn't want our band to be like the guy who hung on too long. I didn't want us to be Willie Mays stumbling after that fly ball or Mickey Mantle seeing his career batting average dip below .300.

We played our final gig together on December 29, 2018, at Proctor's, an intimate theater in Schenectady, New York. Before the last song, I broke the news to the audience. "You get really excited when you start out in this business, but you've got to be smart enough to know when to walk away from it, too," I told them. "I just felt that it's time for me." There was silence at first—I think I kind of caught the concertgoers by surprise—but then they started applauding louder than ever. Even though I knew in my heart the decision was the right one, it's never easy saying good-bye to something you've given heart and soul to for so long. I told them it had been a ball and that I love them very much. Then the band began playing the opening chords to "Midnight Blue." Somehow, we managed not to break down and start crying. Somehow, we held it together and finished on a high note.

• • •

Although I retired my band, I haven't retired from performing. Far from it. In fact, you might say, I'm now playing with four different bands. But, as crazy as that might sound, my schedule is less hectic and more under control than it had been when I was running my own group. I'm playing far fewer gigs. So, you might say I'm easing into retirement down the road; definitely not going cold turkey.

Several years ago, I was approached about doing a Jingle Bell Rock Tour with Eddie Money and Mickey Thomas, the lead singer from Jefferson Starship. They would provide the musicians, and all I would have to do was perform five or six of my songs. I was intrigued by the idea, and it wound up being a lot of fun. We played for about three weeks and sold out most of our shows. Each of us would do individual sets of our original material, then take the stage together for some classic rock Christmas songs.

That wound up leading to more collaborations with rock contemporaries. Lately, I've been doing occasional shows with Asia at a casino in Las Vegas. John Payne from that band had been performing there for some time and would supplement Asia's hits by bringing in well-known singers. He approached me about becoming a regular guest performer. I checked out the show on my computer, and liked what I heard and saw, and have been traveling to Vegas five or six times a year. It's pretty light lifting. You're in and out. You fly in, perform four or five of your hits with some excellent musicians backing you, and you're done.

So, that's one of the four bands I mentioned. I'm also doing a limited number of gigs with the Rock Pack, featuring artists such as former Journey frontman Steve Augeri, Toto lead singer Bobby Kimball, and Tony Lewis from The Outfield. And I'm making a few appearances on the Kings of Chaos Tour. That tour's revolving roster of artists includes me; Dee Snider of Twisted Sister; Gilby Clarke, formerly of Guns N' Roses; and Sebastian Bach, formerly of Skid Road. Fortunately, Foreigner continues to schedule occasional mixed-reunion shows. We're booked for a few more of those in 2019 and 2020. The great thing about all these gigs is that I'm not doing full-throttle, 90-minute-to-two-hour shows, just a handful of songs. I can get to the concerts fairly quickly, so my time away from home is more manageable. And they provide the session players—solid musicians who have experience playing your music.

• • •

When I'm driving in my car, I'll listen to everything from classic rock to current country to new music. I like a lot of what I hear. There are some very talented artists out there. I especially like Adele, the young lady from Britain. She has one of the most distinctive voices I've ever heard. The emotion she puts into her songs is incredible. Sometimes her pronunciation of certain words sounds a little strange, and you have to listen very closely to what's she's saying, but that's cool. She's a huge talent and it has been interesting watching her career unfold.

I enjoy listening to new artists and when I do, I try not to compare them to other artists, past or present. I just try to understand who they want to be. I really enjoy watching shows like *American Idol* and *The Voice*. And, yes, I feel some pride when one of the contestants decides to sing one of my signature songs. I find that a lot of times the rendition is true to form and done very well. Sometimes the singer tries to do crazy things with it, but even if I don't like it, I appreciate what they are trying to do, and my hat's off to them.

Watching those shows reminds me of how fortunate I've been to have had the career I've had. There are so many gifted artists out there, but very few of them ever catch the break you need. I would love to be a judge on one of those shows. I think it would be a ball.

Speaking of people singing my songs, I heard that several actors gave their best Lou Gramm impersonations in the 2012 movie, *Rock of Ages,* which was based on the Broadway musical that was an ode to Eighties rock. Tom Cruise sang "I Want to Know What Love Is," Alec Baldwin did "Juke Box Hero," and Julianne Hough and Diego Boneta performed a duet of "Waiting for a Girl Like You." Having lived the rock star life, I had no desire to go see the movie, so I don't know how good—or bad—their renditions were. Still, it was gratifying that some big-name Hollywood stars were singing songs I had helped make famous, and it was nice to see that several of our tunes made the cut.

They say imitation is the sincerest form of flattery, and I've been blessed to have so many artists list me as one of their early music influences. Among them are Pat Benatar, who wrote in her memoir that her "dream was to be the singer in a rockin' band, like Robert Plant was to Zeppelin or Lou Gramm was to Foreigner." I guess I also had a big impact on American blue-grass country singer Alison Krauss. Every time she plays a venue in western New York, she makes a point of telling the audience "that it's great to be back in the hometown of one of my music idols,

Lou Gramm." By chance, I bumped into Alison in an elevator when she was still a relative unknown, and she told me what a big fan of mine she was and added: "Mr. Gramm, you are going to be hearing about me and my band one day." Well, she was right, and a few years later, I ran into her again after she and her group had hit the big-time. We sat down and had a cup of tea together and chatted about the music business. Again, it's always nice to know your work may have inspired others to pursue their dreams.

People occasionally ask which artists I would have liked to have played with if I could turn back the clock. Two come quickly to mind. One definitely would be John Lennon, whom, as I mentioned, I got to meet and shoot pool with during a happenstance get-together at that New York recording studio back in my Black Sheep days. And a second person would have been Paul Kossoff from the band Free. Kossoff was a blues/rock guitar player who had received classical training from his father. Free featured just a guitar player, a bass player, a drummer, and a singer, but that was more than enough. They never sounded empty. It never failed to excite me when I heard the things Kossoff was doing. Like I said before, I'm so happy I had a chance to see him and his band perform live before his premature death due to a drug overdose back in the early 1970s.

I was a huge Motown fan growing up. I loved the Temptations, the Four Tops, and the Supremes, but my favorite Detroit-city artist probably was Marvin Gaye. I would have loved to have played with him. When I was living in the New York City area I saw him perform at Radio City Music Hall. Man, when he sang, "If This World Were Mine," I got goosebumps. I was such a big fan of his that when I played for the Infirmary, in my early band days, we did that song, along with "Heard It Through the Grapevine" and "How Sweet It Is."

Another guy that influenced me was Paul Rodgers, the lead singer from Free and Bad Company. Jim Taylor, our A&M rep, had turned us on to Free during our Black Sheep days, and Rodgers' pipes captured my attention right away. He had this very emotional voice. He could growl and he could get very soft. At that time in my career, I was still trying to develop my own style. I had just gotten off the drums and I was singing everything in hopes of finding something I could hang my hat on. I was already turned on to Steve Winwood (Traffic) and Steve Marriott (Humble Pie) and, of course, Marvin. But Rodgers had a certain something that was different from the rest of them in the way he approached a song. I didn't make an out-and-out attempt to do everything he did, but, in retrospect, his influence definitely helped me solidify my style.

It also would have been cool to play with Bruce Springsteen, though I did get opportunities to work with his brilliant guitarist, Nils Lofgren, on several occasions, including my solo hit, "Midnight Blue." I met the Boss several years ago after a concert in Rochester. Nils introduced me to him, and we shot the breeze for about a half hour. We talked about our careers, the business, and our kids. He was a very down-to-earth guy. I came away truly amazed about what a rock historian he was. He started naming particulars about this artist and that artist. He told me that he really liked Foreigner's 4 album and songs like "Urgent," "Juke Box Hero," and some of my solo stuff. He was aware of everything I had done. I was extremely impressed how knowledgeable he was about the history of rock 'n' roll. Not all artists are like that, especially Hall-of-Fame musicians like him.

I've been blessed to play with and witness some of the greatest artists of my generation. One of the cool things about Foreigner's success is that it gave us the opportunity to be at mega-concerts with iconic bands. And it also allowed us to see many of our opening acts develop into headliners. You name a group—from the Stones to ELO to Arrowsmith to Santana to KISS to Tom Petty and the Heartbreakers—and we probably played on the same stage at some point.

One time, at a concert in Texas, we were guests of Ozzy Osbourne. Well, we finished our part of the show and were back in our trailers behind the stage getting cleaned up, when we heard the audience screaming hysterically. We stuck our heads out of the windows to see what all the commotion was about. I thought that maybe Ozzy had collapsed on stage. A few moments later, one of the roadies comes back and tells us, "My God, you aren't going to believe this. Ozzy just bit a bat's head off on stage." Now, I've seen and heard a lot of strange things at concerts before, but nothing as bizarre or sick as that. Leave it to Ozzy.

• • •

One group we were constantly compared to was Journey. There was an unspoken rivalry between us, but we wound up getting along well when we toured together in 1999, flip-flopping as headliners, depending on the market we were playing. Steve Perry, the lead singer for many of their hits, was gone by then, and they had brought aboard a sound-alike singer named Steve Augeri. He was a nice kid from Brooklyn and I could see right away that he was struggling mightily with the pressure of trying to replace a legendary performer, so I sort of took him under my wing. He would come to me for advice. "Lou, what should I do about this? And what about that?" He reminded me of my early days with Foreigner, and I was more than happy to help him out.

It was a fun tour. I remember one night in which we opened for them, they were in a tizzy because their drummer had injured himself. So, they asked our drummer if he could fill in. Our guy balked at first, saying, "But I don't know any of your songs that well." During the half hour, while our equipment was being removed and their equipment was being set up, they had him put on a set of headphones so he could listen to one of their previous live shows. He went out there and filled in, and you couldn't tell the difference. He was totally exhausted by the end of the night. Drumming one concert is physically demanding; pulling off a double-header is absolutely crazy.

Although we were together for just a brief period, I had a blast touring with Billy Preston and the Northwest Airlines All-Star Band during the mid-1990s. Preston was a sensational keyboardist, who had played with both the Beatles and Rolling Stones. In fact, he came to be known as the "fifth Beatle." It was a thrill performing with him and getting to know him a little. That band had a stacked roster, featuring guys like Mark Farner (Grand Funk Railroad), Felix Cavaliere (The Rascals), Liberty DeVitto (Billy Joel), Steve Cropper (Booker T and the MG's), and saxophonist Mark Rivera, who played with Foreigner before long stints with Billy Joel and Ringo Starr. We would take turns playing each other's hits. For example, when we were doing The Rascals' hits, I would back up Felix. And when we did Foreigner's hits, he would back me up. Our gigs included the postgame Super Bowl XXXI concert at the New Orleans Superdome and a concert at the tip of Manhattan facing the Statue of Liberty.

Most of the All-Star band members also served as instructors at the first Rock 'n' Roll Fantasy Camp at the Eden Roc Resort & Spa in Miami Beach in April of 1997. The camps were patterned after the fantasy baseball camps that had become the nostalgic rage during the 1980s and were the brainstorm of concert promoter David Fishof and Arkansas entrepreneurs John and Marsha Phillips. For about $3,000 (plus airfare), campers got to participate in what *People* magazine described as "a combination music seminar, backstage party, and open-mike night with the stars." Just like the baseball camps that gave grown men the opportunity to play catch with the likes of Mickey Mantle and Whitey Ford, our camps gave male and female baby boomers a chance to jam with their rock heroes during this four-day session. The price might have seemed a little exorbitant, but as one of the campers told a reporter: "I got no problem with it. To me, it's a bargain."

We had about 45 campers that first year, and some of them were accomplished musicians who were there not only to learn about the nuances of songwriting and performing, but to be discovered. You could sign up for different classes—everything from guitar playing to how to hold an efficient rehearsal. They set up a make-shift recording studio and on Saturday night—the last night of the four-day affair—they held a jam session and sold tickets to the general public for $125, with part of the proceeds benefitting a music therapy foundation. The waiters dressed up like KISS and the spread they put out could have fed several wedding receptions.

I remember singing a duet with a guy who was an audio technician. His knees were knocking at first, but after he harnessed his nerves, he did a great rendition of "Double Vision" with me; he really nailed it. Another guy was a pharmacist from Portland, Oregon, who received this trip as a 45th birthday present from his family. The first night he was out there on stage with me and Nils Lofgren from Bruce Springsteen's E-Street Band we did a rendition of one of my all-time favorite songs, "All Right Now" by Free. The guy looked more excited than a kid on Christmas morning. We didn't need any lighting because his smile lit up the stage. The next day I ran into him at breakfast and he told me,

"You guys are really making us feel comfortable." I thanked him and said, "The way we make a living—that's all that's different between you campers and us rockers."

One of the campers was a celebrity in his own right. His name was Nick Lowery and he had spent a number of years in the National Football League as a kicker for both the Kansas City Chiefs and the New York Jets. Nick said he came to relive his drumming days from his high school/college band called Moonshine. "I really met Mark Farner and Lou Gramm," he said to a reporter, "and they really talked to me as a person and we played together and that was a fantasy come true." Very cool.

I don't believe Fishof made a great deal of money off that first camp, but it did attract quite a bit of national media attention. And he wound up holding another one in New York that July. Years later, the fantasy camps would really take off and be televised on MTV and VH1. It was a lot of fun to participate, and I was impressed with the talent of some of these musicians. I think some of them got breaks as a result of their participation. And the rest of them felt it was money well spent because they got to live out their rock 'n' roll fantasies. A quarter-century later, the fantasy camp continues, and, in another example of my life coming full circle, I recently had another opportunity to be an instructor, along with Aerosmith's Joe Perry and Motley Crue's Vince Neil, at the camp in Vegas.

One of my other current gigs is singing the national anthem at various events. I'm one of the few singers who actually enjoys performing "The Star-Spangled Banner." Many artists don't like singing it because vocally it's a very challenging song. There obviously are scores of stories out there of people botching the lyrics or the notes—everyone from Sinatra to Christine Aguilera in front of a Super Bowl television audience of more than 100 million. And some singers over-stylize it to the point that it doesn't sound the way Francis Scott Key intended it to sound. I've always tried to sing it straight and maintain the song's integrity. I've probably performed it publicly close to 100 times.

Perhaps the biggest event I've ever sung it at was the Indianapolis 500 in 1991. The Brickyard was celebrating its 75th anniversary and there were close to 400,000 people in attendance. I've also performed it before home games involving the Buffalo Bills, Los Angeles Lakers, New York Mets, and New York Rangers. It can be nerve-wracking, especially when you realize there are thousands of people in the stands and millions more watching on television. But I really enjoy it. I'm a patriotic guy and I realize that the anthem sets the tone for the event.

Although I've done thousands of concerts, I still get butterflies before taking the stage. The day those butterflies stop fluttering around in my gut before a performance is the day I'll call it quits. I have certain pre-show rituals I follow. About a half hour before a concert, I'll put on my stage clothes and look for a reasonably quiet place, like a closet or a bathroom, where I can start warming up my voice. I'll go through my low scales and my high scales to get my vocal chords loosened up. Once I'm done doing that, I'll usually get a neck, shoulder, and lower-back massage to remove any muscle tension. Shannon Friend, who was our band's trainer and assistant tour manager for several years, was a registered masseuse. After working on me for about five minutes, I'd be good to go. It's a great way to relieve that pre-concert stress, and I believe it helps me deliver my best performance.

• • •

For the past several years, Billy Joel has played monthly concerts in Madison Square Garden. He's become the arena's musician-in-residence, so to speak, and he often invites guest artists to stop by and perform one or two of their hits. After Mick and I reconciled and performed in one of Foreigner's first reunion concerts, Billy invited us to join him onstage, and we happily accepted, adding our names to a procession of previous distinguished guests that included Paul Simon, John Mellencamp, Sting, Patty Smyth, and Steve Miller.

Madison Square Garden is a special place for musicians. For me, the return was extra special, because I hadn't been back to MSG since that big Atlantic Records anniversary concert nearly three decades earlier. The morning after that bash, I hit rock bottom with my addiction to drugs and alcohol and headed to Hazeltine, Minnesota, for rehab. Blessedly, I have been clean and sober ever since. To return to the Garden in a clearheaded state of mind allowed me to enjoy the moment with a clarity I hadn't had before. The only high I was feeling that evening was from the crowd, which went bonkers when Billy called us onto the stage.

• • •

In 2018, I received a call from my manager telling me that progressive rock musician Alan Parsons wanted to speak to me about a project he was working on. I was familiar with Alan's work, but had never met him. I was intrigued to see what he had in mind. We wound up chatting, and he told me how he had been a fan since my Foreigner days and had admired my vocals and the feeling I put into my songs. He said he was recording a new album (*The Secret*) and wanted me to perform a song of his called "Sometimes." I told him I was flattered but would have to hear it first to make sure it was right for me. He understood completely, and sent me a copy with a test vocal, so I could get an idea for the melody. I listened to it, and was drawn to it immediately.

It was a good song and a challenging song, and that appealed to me because I think it's important for an artist—or anyone for that matter—to occasionally be pushed outside their comfort zone. Although it's string-laden and not something you likely would hear me singing on a Foreigner album or one of my solo albums, I liked it a lot. And I was intrigued about working with Alan. I always respected how pristine and carefully recorded his songs were. And I was well aware he had worked on the production of some of the most iconic albums of all-time, including the Beatles' *Abbey Road* and *Let It Be,* and Pink Floyd's *The Dark Side of Moon.* Several of Alan's songs wound up being played in movies, so the possibility that "Sometimes" might follow suit was enticing, too.

It's always an honor when another artist approaches you to record something. On occasion, I've approached other artists to perform on my albums, and I've had people reach out to me. You just have to make sure it's a good fit and you can do it justice.

• • •

I probably have 16 to 17 notepads filled with ideas for lyrics and melodies. I still have an itch to record some new songs, maybe even produce another album, but I realize it's going to be challenging to pull it off because the music industry has changed so dramatically. The way radio is today, the new artists are on the rock stations and the legacy artists are relegated to classic rock stations where only their old stuff is played. So, it's extremely difficult for artists of my ilk to break out new stuff. You are cut off creatively at the knees.

As a result, there's not much of an incentive to go out and create more because you just don't have the avenues to market it that you once had. Very, very few legacy artists are allowed to reinvent themselves and produce new material. Unless you are a mega-artist with clout like a Bruce Springsteen, you have tremendous difficulty getting the exposure you need. And even someone like Bruce doesn't have the pull he once possessed because the distribution system has changed so drastically and can be difficult to navigate.

I've been particularly bothered by the demise of the album brought about by the music-downloading phenomenon. These days, people just download singles from their favorite artists and never bother to listen to the deep-cut songs the way they did with albums in the old days. For the longest time, albums were structured in such a way that the first song would hook you, the last song on the first side would make you want to turn the album over and listen to the other side, and the grand finale would leave you swooning for more. They were more than just a collection of songs, but rather like a book with a theme, with the songs representing various chapters. There was a strategy involved, with a mix of songs—a couple of rockers here, a ballad there. People would hear the hits on the radio, which would prompt them to buy the album, and, invariably, they would listen to the deep cuts, and would wind up liking those songs as much as if not better than the hits. Sadly, those days are gone.

I realize that if I still want to play the game, I'm going to have to adapt to the new rules. I'm preparing to release some new—and remastered—material for download in the not-so-distant future. Back in the days when I did my solo albums, I put 10–12 songs on an album. There were probably two or three extras that were almost done, but didn't make the cut. So, between my two solo albums and *Shadow King*, which was a collaboration between me and current Dep Leppard guitarist Vivian Campbell, there's another album's worth of songs I've been massaging. What I'm hoping to do is make three songs available at a time. We'll release them, market them, and monitor the downloads. And once the downloads and sales begin to subside—say after two or three months—we'll release another three songs. Perhaps, after releasing all 10, we might put them together on a CD, complete with an artsy album cover and liner notes about the songs and artists. I'm also exploring the possibility of compiling a greatest hits album of my non-Foreigner stuff. People have asked me to include some of my Foreigner music, too, and I would love to, but legally I'm prevented from doing that because I don't own the rights. Hopefully, the release of my individual stuff will generate a bunch of interest, and maybe even prompt me to produce more new material. Stay tuned.

• • •

In the spring of 2019, Mick and I headed to Toronto for the premiere of a musical, titled *Juke Box Hero*. Mick and Foreigner management gave the writers and producers permission to use about 20 songs. I thought the plot, which centers around two brothers—one a guitar player, the other a vocalist—felt kind of cliché, like a soap opera. The critics were much crueler in their assessments than I was. Let's just say, the musical needed a lot of work. The directors were hoping to use the Toronto kickoff as a springboard for an Off-Broadway tour and eventually a stint on Broadway, but from what I understand, the show's been at least temporarily shut down.

Through the years, there have been some discrepancies about the origins of the song "Juke Box Hero." I'd like to clear those up. Some have claimed that a young man who was standing outside one of Foreigner's concerts in Cincinnati was the inspiration for the song. That's not true. The song definitely is autobiographical, with a few creative factual digressions here and there. It was inspired by my own experiences as a teenager, getting drenched in the rain, near the backstage door of the Rochester War Memorial. I didn't have a ticket to that night's Jimi Hendrix concert, but I still was able to get a feel for the concert from the periphery. Every time the security guard opened the door to let in people who had backstage passes, I'd stick my head in and I'd see Jimi playing for about 10 to 15 seconds before the door closed again. Even with it shut, I could hear Hendrix's guitar pulsating and screeching through the walls—that's how loudly he was playing. And I vividly remember hearing the thunderous roar of the crowd each time he reached a crescendo or was starting or ending a new song. That concert wound up being even crazier than imagined, because some wacked-out kids started lighting seat padding on fire.

Although I was soaked from the rain, that concert, which I guess you could say I kind of attended, made an indelible impression—an impression that years later prompted me to write about the experience. "Juke Box Hero" is a song about being beaten down, but not enough to stop dreaming and hoping. I started writing the lyrics about this teenager without a ticket to a sold-out show standing in the wind and the rain outside a concert. I had him fantasizing, just as I had, about being on that stage someday. And I changed the plot, so the kid would dream about playing a guitar rather than the drums because it was a better fit with the melody I was composing simultaneously with the lyrics. I took the song to a certain point, then brought it to Mick. He was extremely enthused about it, and helped me tweak it some more. Of all the songs I've written and performed, that remains one of my proudest. It's become a rock classic and I think it really put to rest any questions about whether Foreigner was capable of delivering a hard rock song.

• • •

I've performed thousands of concerts in my life, so, understandably, most of them blur together. But some are still vivid all these decades later. Few more so than the Foreigner concert we did on April 27, 1978, at the Rainbow Theatre in London. And, thanks to the recent discovery of original film reels from that concert, our fans and I have been able to relive those youthful days when we exploded onto the scene and rocketed up the charts. Nearly four decades later, those reels were remixed and remastered and released on DVD and made available on CD as a double album set. A noted filmmaker from England began following us while we were out promoting our debut album in America, and decided to shoot us from a bunch of different angles when we headed across the pond to perform at the Rainbow— one of the music world's most revered concert halls. The DVD, titled *Foreigner: Live at the Rainbow '78,* really captures the youthful vibrancy and energy we had back in the day. Watching it was a trip—a trip back in time. I couldn't help but notice how young we looked and—please pardon the boasting—how good we sounded.

There's clearly a different vibe between your studio recordings and your live performances. You can become a little more reckless and interpretative with the songs at concerts, and I like that. They get a little looser and a little more fun to play. Plus, you get to play off the energy of the audience, and there's nothing that can simulate that stimulation.

As I watched the DVD, I also noticed how I hopped up next to Dennis Elliott and began banging on a second set of drums for the songs "Starrider" and "Headknocker." It was a blast returning to my roots as a drummer, and I would do that from time-to-time during our concerts. I am so thrilled someone rediscovered the films of this concert and released them. They clearly show us at the peak of the band's musical powers.

While doing an interview with Rock Cellar about the

release of *Live at the Rainbow,* I was told about a re-discovered BBC Radio One interview with George Harrison and Michael Jackson in which they reviewed one of our Foreigner hits, "Blue Morning, Blue Day." The interviewer told me that George and Michael each gave it a "thumbs up," said they really enjoyed it. How cool is that?

• • •

While in Toronto for the musical premiere of *Juke Box Hero,* Mick and I sat down with former CBS news anchor Dan Rather for our first joint interview in about 20 years. Rather has been focusing on rock artists for his cable television show, *The Big Interview,* and had thought this setting would be ideal because it would be more relaxed than it would have been were we preparing for one of our reunion concerts. I thought Rather did a decent job getting us to talk about our triumphs and difficulties. At one point, he asked how we became estranged. "I think when we supposed to be at our creative best, which was when we were writing songs, there seemed to be either miscommunication or, sometimes, no communication at all," I answered. "Someone would end up at the end of a day or two very unfulfilled, and you'd start putting a wall up. You're supposed to be writing songs, but at the end of the day you would have accomplished nothing. There'd be resentment and anger. Pretty soon you wouldn't bother to get together to write songs because you knew the way it was going to be and that's kind of what happened to us at a certain point."

During the interview, Mick seemed more candid and contrite than I had seen him before. "I felt I wasn't really in control, and I let myself go a bit," he told Rather. "That's part of the reason we lost touch. And I look back at that with regret because that does a number on you. I think we could have carried on and seen where our friendship would have gone."

I thought Mick was spot-on talking about the pressure we both felt to keep producing highly successful albums. We had sprinted out of the blocks so fast, with our self-titled debut album selling five million copies. Remarkably, we had four multi-platinum albums in our first four tries. We were on an incredible roll, but, in the process, had created a monster. And we had to keep feeding that monster or it would eat us up. It was a pace no artist could maintain, and I think that pressure eventually got to each of us, and wrecked our friendship. The Rather interview was a confessional in some respects, and I saw a vulnerable side to Mick that I hadn't witnessed before.

• • •

Not long after Robyn and I were married, she asked me if I would ever consider becoming a father again. She had come from a close-knit Italian-American family and always wanted to have children but had never found herself in the right relationship for that to happen. Her initial inquiry caught me a little off-guard. Don't get me wrong. I dearly loved being a dad, but I already had four kids and was a little concerned about bringing a child into this world at my age. You start doing the math and begin wondering if you are going to be around for the seminal moments in that child's life. Heck, I would be in my eighties, God-willing, by the time that child graduated from high school.

But the more I thought about it, the more I wanted to do this—for Robyn and for us. And I'm so happy we did. These journeys are rarely straight lines, and we faced some heartache along the way as Robyn suffered some miscarriages. During her last pregnancy, her doctor instructed her to take it really easy. No running up and down the stairs. No heavy lifting. Robyn followed his advice to a T, and carried full-term. Luciana's birth was one of the greatest moments of our lives. When little "Lucci" came out, I couldn't believe my eyes. I said, "Look, Robyn, she has your hair; she's a redhead!" And Robyn joked, "Oh, no, that poor girl."

I no longer worry about whether I'm going to be around for Lucci's milestone moments. That's in God's hands. No one, regardless of age, is guaranteed tomorrow, so I try to enjoy every day to the fullest. And what joy this ball of fire has brought me and Robyn. Lucci is as smart as a whip and is constantly making us smile. She likes to dance and sing along to the educational cartoon characters on television. So what if her lyrics are gibberish? She definitely has a little of the performer gene in her. She'll look over to make sure we are watching as she moves to the rhythm of the beat. Sorry to be the doting dad here, but she's so adorable.

• • •

I'm happy to report that I'm feeling better physically and mentally than I have in a long time, and each year things improve. I exercise with a trainer several days a week and maintain a fairly strict diet, so I've been able to shed more than 100 pounds of the weight I gained as a result of the destruction of my pituitary gland and the steroids I was required to take. I'm never going to be the taut, 145-pounder I was before the surgery, but I'm in a much, much healthier place than I was the first six, seven years while I was recuperating from the surgery. And my memory, voice, and creativity also have bounced back, so I feel truly blessed.

People have asked me how I would like to be remembered musically. It's a difficult question. I don't know if I have a good answer. I guess I would hope to be remembered as a rock vocalist who sang and wrote with a lot of soul and feeling. I'd like to be remembered as a rock singer, not a ballad singer, even though I enjoyed doing ballads from time to time. It does strike me as funny that the two songs I'm most remembered for are ballads— "I Want to Know What Love Is" and "I've Been Waiting for a

Girl Like You." I understand that those songs gave me a great opportunity to showcase the full range of my voice, to become, in the words of *Rolling Stone* magazine, "the Pavarotti of the power ballad," and to prompt some music reviewers to call my pipes operatic. And I'm often told that women, in particular, absolutely love those songs and that guys loved 'em, too, because it gave them openings to slow dance with their ladies. I'm flattered by that and I'm not complaining that I did those songs—they were great songs. But I'm a rocker to the core, and unfortunately those two ballads overshadow so many other good songs we did. If they hadn't been made people might see some of those other classic songs in a different light. I still sing those ballads at my concerts and I sing them with all the soul and feeling I can muster, but, to be honest, I enjoy singing rockers like "Urgent," "Juke Box Hero" and "Midnight Blue" much more.

Looking back, I would hope that people thought my voice was distinctive, that I had not only a good set of pipes, but also a good sense of what my place was in the song—that I didn't try to over-sing it or under-sing it. That would be important to me. I know there are a lot of "top this" or "top that" lists out there. I genuinely can't begin to tell you where I stand compared to this singer or that singer. That's for others to decide. You can go crazy if you allow yourself to get caught up in that stuff.

I mentioned several times how I feel the critics haven't been overly kind to Foreigner through the years. That bothers me, but I've come to realize there's nothing you can do about those things. Ultimately you are judged by rock 'n' roll fans. They are the critics who truly matter. And nearly 80 million record sales and thousands of sold-out concerts later, I guess you can say they've spoken rather loudly. That dozens of the songs we composed are still being played today around the clock and around the world is an indication that we created a body of work that has stood the test of time. And I couldn't be more grateful for our fans loyal support through the decades. It's meant the world to me because, without them, this working-class kid from Rochester, New York, never could have taken this incredible rock 'n' roll journey.

—June 2019

Lou Gramm's Discography

Lou Gramm's contributions as a singer and songwriter with Foreigner and his own band resulted in six multi-platinum albums and 21 Top 40 singles. Six albums he was involved with broke into the top 10, eight into the top 50, and nine into the top 100. *Double Vision* has sales exceeding 7 million as does a greatest hits album released in 2002. The 4 LP has surpassed sales of 6 million and Foreigner's self-titled debut and *Head Games* albums have eclipsed the 5 million mark.

Along the way, Lou contributed to 11 Top 10 singles and 27 Top 100 singles.

His solo single, "Midnight Blue," peaked at No. 5 in 1987 and received the most radio play of any record that year, edging, among others, U2's seminal hit, "I Still Haven't Found What I'm Looking For."

Lou's powerful vocals helped catapult Foreigner's "I Want to Know What Love Is" to the top of the *Billboard* charts in the United States and United Kingdom in 1987.

According to the Recording Industry Association of America, Foreigner ranks 40th all-time in records sold. Toss in Lou's solo work and he's been involved in the sales of more than 80 million records.

Here's a look at Lou's albums and singles and where they ranked in the United States, United Kingdom, and Germany:

Solo Albums
  Ready or Not (1987) No. 27 US
  Long Hard Look (1989) No. 85 US
  Lou Gramm Band (2009)

Hit Solo Singles
  "Midnight Blue" (1987) No. 5 US; No. 82 UK
  "Ready or Not" (1987) No. 54
  "Just Between You and Me" (1989) No. 6 US
  "True Blue Love" (1989) No. 40 US

Albums with Foreigner
  Foreigner (1977) No. 4 US
  Double Vision (1978) No. 3 US; No. 32 UK
  Head Games (1979) No. 5 US
  4 (1981) No. 1 US for 10 weeks; No. 5 UK
  Records (1982) No. 10 US; No. 58 UK
  Agent Provocateur (1984) No. 4 US; No. 1 UK
  Inside Information (1987) No. 15 US; No. 64 UK
  The Very Best of… (1992)
  The Very Best of… and Beyond (1992) No. 123 US; No. 19 UK
  Classic Hits Live/Best of (1993)
  Juke Box Heroes: The Best of (1994)
  Mr. Moonlight (1994) No. 136 US; No. 59 UK
  The Platinum Collection (1999)

Rough Diamonds No. 1 (1999)
Hot Blooded and Other Hits (2000)
Anthology: Juke Box Heroes (2000)
Complete Greatest Hits (2002) No. 80 US
The Definitive (2002) No. 33 UK
No End in Sight: The Very Best of Foreigner (2008)

Hit Singles with Foreigner

"Feels Like the First Time" (1977) No. 4 US; No. 39 UK
"Cold As Ice" (1977) No. 6 US; No. 24 UK
"Long, Long Way From Home" (1978) No. 20 US
"Hot Blooded" (1978) No. 3 US; No. 42 UK
"Double Vision" (1978) No. 2 US
"Blue Morning, Blue Day" (1979) No. 15 US; No. 45 UK
"Dirty White Boy" (1979) No. 12 US
"Head Games" (1979) No. 14 US
"Women" (1980) No. 41
"Urgent" (1981) No. 4 US; No. 54 UK; No. 12 Germany
"Waiting for a Girl Like You" (1981) No. 2 US; No. 8 UK;
    No. 29 Germany
"Juke Box Hero" (1981) No. 26 US; No. 48 UK; No. 24
    Germany
"Break It Up" (1982) No. 26 US
"Luanne" (1982) No. 75 US
"I Want to Know What Love Is" (1984) No. 1 US and UK;
    No. 3 Germany
"That Was Yesterday" (1985) No. 12 US; No. 28 UK; No.
    31 Germany
"Reaction to Action" (1985) No. 54 US
"Down On Love" (1985) No. 54

"Say You Will" (1987) No. 6 US; No. 71 UK; No. 22
Germany

"I Don't Want to Live Without You" (1988) No. 5 US; No.
91 UK

"Heart Turns to Stone" (1988) No. 56 US

"With Heaven on Our Side" (1991) No. 103 US

"Until the End of Time" (1994) No. 42 US

Albums with Black Sheep

S/T (1975)

Encouraging Words (1975)

Albums with Poor Heart

Foreigner in a Strange Land (1988)

The Best of the Early Years (1993)

Albums with Shadow King

Shadow King (1991)

Albums with Liberty N' Justice

Welcome to the Revolution (2001)

Albums with Don Mancuso

D: Drive (2005)

Breakdown:

Albums: 9 Top 100s; 8 Top 50s; 6 Top 10s

Singles: 27 Top 100s; 21 Top 40s; 11 Top 10s

Awards and Nominations

1977: *Billboard* magazine's choice for Top New Artist

1977: Grammy nomination for Best New Artist

1979: People's Choice Award in Favorite Song category for "Double Vision"

1981: Grammy nomination for Best Rock Performance by a Duo or Group

1983: Canadian Juno nomination for Best International Artist

1984: Grammy nomination in Best Album category for 4

1985: Grammy nomination for Best Rock Performance by a Duo or Group for "I Want to Know What Love Is"

1985: Canadian Juno Award in Best Song Category for "I Want to Know What Love Is"

1992: Charter Inductee of the Monroe Community College Alumni Hall of Fame

2011: Inductee of the Gates Chili High School Alumni Hall of Fame

2011: Charter Inductee of the Rochester Music Hall of Fame

2013: Songwriters Hall of Fame inductee

Sources

Books

All-Music Guide to Rock: The Definitive Guide to Rock, Pop and Soul. Ann Arbor, Mich.: All Media Guide, 2002.

Rolling Stone Album Guide: The Definitive Guide to the Best of Rock, Pop, Rap, Jazz, Blues, Country, Soul, Folk & Gospel. New York: Random House, 1992.

The Billboard Book of Top 40 Hits. New York: Billboard Books, an imprint of Watson-Guptill Publications, 1989.

Rees, Dafydd, and Luke Crampton. *The Encyclopedia of Rock Stars.* New York: DK Publishing, Inc., 1996.

George-Warren, Holly, and Patricia Romanowski, eds. *The Rolling Stone Encyclopedia of Rock & Roll,* third edition. New York: Rolling Stone Press, 2001.

The Rolling Stone Illustrated History of Rock 'N' Roll. New York: Random House, 1992.

Newspapers & Magazines

Bandvista: Smashing Interviews Magazine

Billboard

Buffalo News

Christgau's Record Guide

City Newspaper (Rochester, N.Y.)

Cleveland Plain-Dealer

Dallas Morning News

El-Paso Times

Free Time Magazine

Hartford Courant
Huntsville Times
Italian-American Community
   News
Los Angeles Daily News
Los Angeles Times
The Miami Herald
Knight-Ridder Newspapers
Music Collectors Magazine
New York Times
Newsday
Palm Beach Post
Pasadena Star-News
People Magazine
Pittsburgh Post-Gazette

Pittsburgh Tribune
Rochester (N.Y.) Democrat &
   Chronicle
Rochester (N.Y.) Times-Union
Rolling Stone Magazine
San Diego Union-Tribune
Super Rock Magazine
Syracuse Herald-Journal
Syracuse Post-Standard
Toronto Globe & Mail
Toronto Star
Upstate Magazine
Variety magazine
The Washington Post

Websites

atlanticrecords.com
capitolrecords.com
elyrics.net
Examiner.com
Foreigner.com
goldminemag.com
lou-gramm.com
people.com
rockshowcritique.com
smashinginterviews.com

softshoe-slim.com
songlyrics.com
spinner.com
thedailybeast.com
ultimateclassicrock.com
utopiaartists.com
youtube.com
Wikipedia.org
4reigner.net

Miscellaneous

Other sources included Steve Dollar, Foreigner concert programs, publicity materials and albums, Bob Gallino, Jack Garner, Ben Grammatico, Robyn Grammatico, Lou Gramm's scrapbooks and solo albums, Champ Harnish, Barbara Isaacs, Claudette James, Dave Kane, Phil Marder, Stephen Monroe, Brian Moran, MTV, Rock 'N Roll Hall of Fame, Andy Smith, Jeff Spevak, Dave Stearns, Jim Trowbridge, and VH1.

Index

19th Ward, 3

A

AC/DC, 56, 99, 101, 190
Adams, Bryan, 114
Adele, 196
Aerosmith, 114, 118, 161, 209
Agent Provocateur, 109, 111, 114-15, 119, 121, 148, 224
Aguilera, Christina, 209
Albany, New York, 43
"All Right Now," 22, 32, 79, 208
American Bandstand, 146
American Idol, 22, 203
American University, 70
Animals, The, 19, 24, 26
AOR, 71, 81
Aqua Teen Hunger Force, 66
Arkansas, 207
Atlantic Records, 22, 52, 55, 62, 81, 83, 96, 99-101, 108-9, 123, 127, 134-35, 143, 147, 189
Auditorium Theater, 47
Augeri, Steve, 160, 202
Australia, 88, 148, 150, 177

B

Bad Company, 40, 205
Baker, Roy Thomas, 92-95
Baldwin, Alec, 203
Baltimore Orioles, 5

Beatles, The, 13-14, 18-22, 24, 27, 53, 71, 104, 108, 130, 207, 212
Beck, John, 6-7
Behind The Music, 131
Belgium, 88, 106
Bella Donna, 104
Belushi, John, 66
Benatar, Pat, 104, 203
Berlin, 177
Betty Ford Center, 170
Betty Ford Clinic, 140
Bice, Bo, 22
Big Apple, 64, 84, 152
Billboard, 35, 75, 78, 89, 105, 108
Black, Dr. Peter, xii-xiii, 152-53, 156, 160
Black Sheep, 85, 126, 128, 136, 149, 166-67, 169, 171, 174, 197, 204-05, 226
"Blue Morning, Blue Day," 83, 217
Blue Oyster Cult, 176
Blue Tones, 7
Bon Jovi, Jon, 161
Bonafede, Mike, 166
Boneta, Diego, 203
Bonham, John, 107
Booker T and the MGs, 207
Boston, xii-xiii, 42, 45, 62, 95, 152
Bowie, David, 190
Boys Lie, 166
Brass Buttons, 32
Brass Rail, 33

"Break It Up," 225
Brickyard, 210
Brigham & Women's Hospital, xiii, 152, 154, 160
Bright Eyes Fund, 167
British Invasion, 19, 32
British Walkers, 14
Broadway, 203
Brooklyn, 206
Brooklyn Dodgers, 4-6
Brown, Charlie, 156
Brown, James, 39, 191
Brubek, Dave, 7
Buffalo, 22, 29, 31, 34, 84
Buffalo Bills, 6, 84, 210
Buick LeSabre, 182
Buick Turbo-T, 186
Burdon, Eric, 26
Burger King, 67
Butch, 24, 183
Butera, Robyn, 178
Buziak, Bob, 42

C

Cal-Jam, 79
Cal-Jam II, 84
Camaro, 186
Campanella, Roy, 4
Campbell, Vivian, 136
"Can You Hear Me Calling?", 39
Canada, 52, 106
Canadian Juno, 227
Canandaigua, 21
Capitol Records, 20, 36, 38, 41, 44, 47
Cartoon Network, The, 66
Cars, The, 62, 92
Caruso, 2
Cash, Johnny, 9
Catch 22, 166
Cavaliere, Felix, 207
Cavern Club, The, 21
"Chain On Me," 38
Chapman, John David, 20
Charles, Ray, 24
Charlotte, 183
Charter Inductee, 227
Cheap Trick, 62, 145

Chevy, 181, 184-85
Chili Grange, 24
CHiPs, 88
Chrysalis Records, 36-38
Cinderella, 136
Citi Field, 5
Civil War, 28, 155
Clark, Dick, 146
Clash, The, 62
Classic Hits Live/Best of, 224
Cleveland, 43, 60
Climax Blues Band, 38
Cocker, Joe, 21, 32
"Cold As Ice," 66, 102, 190-191, 225
Collins, Phil, 135-36
Columbia, 38
Comeback Tour, 160
Complete Greatest Hits, 225
Connecticut, 35
Cooper, Alice, 190
Crispin Cioe, 126
Crosby, Stills & Nash, 190
Cross, Christopher, 22
Crow, Sheryl, 145
Crozier, Larry, 31, 41, 166
Cruise, Tom, 203
"Cuts Like A Knife," 114

D

Daltrey, Roger, 107
Danbury State Prison, 35
Davidson, John, 77-78
Davis, Bette, 66
Death Valley, 71
Def Leppard, 99-101
DeVitto, Liberty, 207
Dion and The Belmonts, 8-9
"Dirty White Boy," 118, 145, 225
DJ, 8, 60-61, 79
Dodge Charger, 183
Dolby, Thomas, 100, 105
Dollar, Steve, 125
Donnie Iris and the Cruisers, 136
Donny, Tony & the Knighthawks, 23
Doobie Brothers, 69-70, 73, 81, 127
Doo-Wop, 8, 24
Dorsey Brothers, 8

Double Vision, 29, 78, 83-84, 92, 96, 102, 136, 149, 193, 223-24
"Double Vision," x, 67, 76, 88, 208, 225, 227
"Down On Love," 225
Dr. Hook, 22
"Dream Weaver," 54
Dugay, Ron, 78
Duke of Flatbush, 5
Dylan, Bob, 84, 191

E

E Street Band, 122
Earth, Wind & Fire, 38, 152
Eastman Kodak Company, 6
Eastman School of Music, 6
Eastman, George, 6
Ebbets Field, 5
Eddy, Chuck, 149
Eden Roc Resort & Spa, 207
Edgar Winter Group, 22
Edwards, Johnny, 143
"Eight Days A Week," 21
Electric Light Orchestra (ELO), 40, 206
Elliott, Dennis, 52-54, 57, 63, 65, 83, 196
Ellis Island, 2
Emerick, Geoff, 22
England, 16, 72, 87, 106, 110, 171
Erbe, 3
Escape, 14, 104
Esposito, Phil, 78
Estrada, Erik, 88
E Street Band, 122
Europe, 29, 53, 83, 88, 106, 121, 143, 148, 150, 177-78
Everly Brothers, 8-9

F

Fab Four, 18
Far East, 83, 88
Farner, Mark, 207, 209
Favorite Song, 208
"Feeling All Right," 32
"Feels Like The First Time," xi, 50, 59, 63, 69-71, 173, 191, 225
Fire, Tom, 31

Fishof, David, 207
Fitzgerald, Ella, 8
Flack, Roberta, 21
Fleetwood Mac, 62, 79, 84, 92, 190
Florida, 145
Flying Wallendas, 84
Ford Galaxie, 39, 71
Foreigner, x-xi, 5, 18, 20-22, 29, 50, 52-53, 55, 57, 59, 62-64, 66-67, 69, 75, 83-88, 96, 98-99, 101-3, 107, 109, 111, 113, 116, 118, 120-29, 131-36, 141, 143-45, 147-50, 152, 155-56, 160, 165-66, 169-72, 174-75, 184-85, 189-98, 202-07, 211-217, 220, 223-26, 230
Foreigner in a Strange Land, 226
Four Tops, The, 204
Frampton, Peter, 84, 97, 126
France, 88, 106
Frankie Goes To Hollywood, 110
Franklin High School, 1
Franklin, Aretha, 22, 56, 191
Free, 7, 19, 22, 32, 34, 70, 79, 131, 136, 204-05, 208
Friend, Shannon, 210
Fudge, Vanilla, 105

G

Gagliardi, Ed, 54, 57, 63, 65, 96
Galli-Campi, Amri, 74-75
Gallo, Joe, 25
Garner, Jack, 33, 86
Gates Chili High School, 28, 118
Gates Chili High School Alumni Hall of Fame, 227
Gaudio, Ma, 25-26
Gaudio, Tony, 25
Gaye, Marvin, 22, 204
Generama, 148
Genesee Valley Park, 4
Genesis, 136
Georgetown, 70
Goldmine, 189, 230
Golisano Children's Hospital, 167
Graham, Bill, 79

Grammatico, Ben, 3, 7-12, 116, 126, 182, 197, 230
Grammatico, Ben, Sr., 8, 14, 87
Grammatico, Joe, 164, 167, 171
Grammatico, Matt, 164
Grammatico, Natalie, 164, 167, 171
Grammatico, Nick, 164
Grammatico, Nikki, 1, 14, 87
Grammatico, Roseanne, 93
Grand Funk Railroad, 207
Gray, Joel, 74
Green, Al, 21
Greenberg, Jerry, 99
Greenwood, Al, 49, 51, 54, 57, 63, 65, 98, 184, 195
Gretsch, 10
Grosvenor, Luther, 47
GTO, 183

H

Hagar, Sammy, 123
Hallyday, Johnny, 53
Hamptons, 161
Hansen, Kelly, 189-90
Harrison, George, 21, 53, 217
Hawkins, Edwin, 112
Hazelden Treatment Center, 138-42, 146, 164, 172
"Head Games," 225
Head Games, 92, 96-97, 99, 101-2, 184, 222, 224
"Headknocker," 87
"Heard It Through the Grapevine," 204
Heart, 81-82
"Heart Turns to Stone," 210
Hendrix, Jimi, 105
Hodges, Gil, 4
Holly, Buddy, 9, 106
Hollywood, 88, 94, 129
Hong Kong, 88
"Honky Tonk Woman," 79
Horn, Trevor, 110
"Hot Blooded," 78-79, 81, 83, 102, 118, 173, 196
Hot Rod, 185
Hough, Julianne, 203
"Hound Dog," 8-9, 37

"How Sweet It Is," 204
Humble Pie, 19, 22, 32, 34, 205
"Hungry Heart," 108
Hunter, Ian, 135

I

"I Don't Want To Live Without You," 119, 121, 226
"I Still Haven't Found What I'm Looking For," 124, 222
"I Want To Know What Love Is," v, 48, 50, 80, 109-110, 112-13, 115, 118-19, 126, 130, 135, 145, 148, 182, 192, 196, 203, 219, 222, 225
"If This World Were Mine," 204
Indianapolis 500, 210
Inside Information, 119-21, 131, 148, 224

J

Jacksons, 113
Jacobs, Jeff, 149
Jagger, Mick, 13, 15-16, 60, 111
James, Harry, 8
Japan, x, 88, 148, 150, 152, 174, 177-78
Jefferson Starship, 201
Jesus Christ, 142, 172
Jingle Bell Rock tour, 201
Joel, Billy, 135, 149
John Wayne Airport, 143
Jones, Brian, 17
Jones, John Paul, 53, 72
Jones, Kevin, 176
Jones, Mick, viii, 47-48, 55, 57-58, 63, 66, 72, 77, 80, 83, 85, 87-88, 92-99, 101-3, 105-6, 110-12, 114-16, 119-25, 127-28, 130-32, 135-36, 138, 141, 143-46, 149, 152, 155, 190
Journey, 104, 160, 190, 192, 202, 206
"Juke Box Hero," viii, xii, xiv, 104-5, 111, 118, 140, 157, 190, 192, 203, 205, 214-15, 220, 225
Juke Box Heroes: The Best of Foreigner, 147, 224
"Just Between You and Me," 135, 186, 224

K

Kalodner, John, 55
Kansas, 176
Kansas City, 38, 83
Kansas City Chiefs, 209
Kennedy, John F., 28
Keuka Lake, 155
Key, Francis Scott, 210
King Crimson, 54
King, B.B., 21
King, Rodney, 144
Kingsmen, The, 10
Kinks, 19
KISS, 41-44, 85, 161, 206, 208
KLOS, 60
Knight, Holly, 135
Knoll, Andy, 172, 192, 197
Koladner, John, 100
Kossoff, Paul, 22, 204
Koufax, Sandy, 4
Krauss, Alison, 203
Kuala Lumpur, 88

L

Lacey, Liam, 107
Laine, Denny, 22
Lake Avenue, 183-84
Lake Ontario, 183
"Land of the Rising Sun," 24
Lange, Robert John "Mutt," 99-100
Las Vegas, 195, 201
LAX, 94, 143
Led Zeppelin, 53, 57, 60, 107, 190
Lennon, John, 19-21, 56, 60, 111, 190, 191, 204
Leno, Jay, 186
Leo, Kid, 60
LeSabre, 182
"Let It Be," 170
"Let Me Be Your Love-Maker, Let Me Be Your Soul-Shaker," 80
Liberty N' Justice, 226
Lincoln Zephyr, 32
Little League, 4, 165
Live With Regis and Kathie Lee, 146
Liverpool, 21
Lloyd, Ian, 54, 135

Lofgren, Nils, 21, 122, 126, 205, 208
Lombard, William, 15
London, 87-88
Long Distance Voyager, 104
Long Hard Look, 135, 224
Long Island, 54, 161
"Long, Long Way From Home," v, 47, 63, 145, 225
Los Angeles, 5, 60, 71, 110, 121, 133, 143
Los Angeles Forum, 104
Los Angeles Lakers, 210
Los Angeles Times, 98, 128
Lost Boys, The, 129
"Lost in the Shadows," 129
Lou Gramm: The Early Years, 29
Lou Gramm Band, 136, 172, 197, 224
"Love Is Alive," 54
Love, Stuart Alan, 38, 42
Lowery, Nick, 209
"Luanne," 106, 225
"Lucille," 107
Lyons, Gary, 92

M

Madison, 1, 21, 77-78, 84, 134
Madison High School, 1
Madison Square Garden, 21, 77-78, 84, 134
"Magic Man," 81
Maloney, Don, 78
Mancuso, Don, 32, 37, 40, 114, 126, 166, 172, 197, 226
Manhattan, 49, 52, 54, 64, 74, 78, 131, 133, 196
Manhattan Museum of Art, 196
Marder, Phil, 230
Marriott, Steve, 205
Marty, 161
Masetta, Nikki, 1
Mason, Dave, 33
McCartney, Paul, 19, 21, 111, 150, 191
McDonald and Giles, 54
McDonald, Ian, 49, 53-54, 63, 65, 98, 195
McDonald, Michael, 69, 170
McVan's, 34

Metropolitan Opera, 74
Mets, 5, 76, 196
Mexico City, 169
Miami, 39
Miami Beach, 207
Michigan, 39, 72, 176
Middleton, Barry, 28
"Midnight Blue," 21, 121-24, 128, 186, 190, 200, 205, 220, 223-24
Miller, Steve, 131-32
Minnelli, Liza, 74
Minnesota, 138, 140
Mississippi Queen, 56
Money, Eddie, 201
Monk, Thelonious, 7
Monroe Community College, 27-28, 199
Monroe Community College Alumni Hall of Fame, 227
Monroe County Public Safety Building, 45
Montreal, 16
Moody Blues, The, 104
Moonshine, 209
Morris, Doug, 123
Motown, 22, 204
Mount Olivet Baptist Church Mass Choir, 118
Mountain, 56
Mr. Moonlight, 147-50, 224
MTV, 130-31, 209
Muni, Scott, 60
Munich, 107, 177
Music Lovers, 6

N

National Anthem, 5, 78, 84, 209
Neisner's, 10
Netherlands, 169-70
New Jersey Mass Choir, 112
New Orleans Superdome, 207
New York City, 35, 37, 48, 52, 60, 174, 192, 197, 204
New York International, 185
New York Jets, 209
New Zealand, 88
Newcombe, Don, 4

Newman, Paul, 185
Nicks, Stevie, 104
Night of the Prom tour, 169
Night Life, 104
No End In Sight: The Very Best of Foreigner, 225
Northwest Airlines All-Star Band, 207
Norton Street, 118
Norway, 189
Not Where They Came From, 62
Nudestock, 176
Nugent, Ted, 38

O

"Oh, Happy Day," 112
Ohio, 38
Olds 442, 184, 186
Olsen, Keith, 92, 136
Ono, Yoko, 20, 126
Orange Monkey, 33, 35
Oregon, 202
Orpheum Theater, 42
Osbourne, Ozzy, 206
Ossining, 52

P

Page, Jimmy, 53, 60, 107, 135
Paris, 53, 111
Penny Arcade, 33
People's Choice Award, 88, 227
Perry, Steve, 160, 206
PHFTT, 25, 27
Philadelphia, 18, 77, 84
Philadelphia Flyers, 77-78
Philbin, Regis, 146
PJ's Bar, 23
Plant, Robert, 107, 197
Platinum Collection, The, 224
Pointer Sisters, 170
Pointer, Bonnie, 170
Pontiac, 8, 180
Poor Heart, 28-31, 226
Prager, Bud, 51, 56, 61, 81, 120
Precious Time, 104
Presley, Elvis, 8
Preston, Billy, 207
"Prisoner of Love," 145

Procol Harum, 36-37
Pullaro, Joe, 28

Q

Queen, 92-93
Quincy Market, 154

R

Radio City Music Hall, 204
Ralph, Mick, 40
Rangers, 77-78, 210
Rascals, The, 207
Raspberries, 40
"Reaction to Action," 81, 225
Ready Steady Go!, 130
Record Plant, 37, 39
Recording Industry Association of
    America, 223
Red, White & Blue Band, 32
Red Wings, 119
Reese, PeeWee, 4
Regna, Tom, 26
"Rev on the Red Line," 184-85
RFK Stadium, 18, 84
Rhythm Safari, 148
Rich Stadium, 84
Richard, Little, 9
Richards, Keith, 16,111
Rivera, Mark, 126
Robinson, Jackie, 4
Rocco, Ron, 31, 41
Rochester (NY), xi, 1-3, 6-7, 10, 12, 15,
    17, 21-23, 26-29, 31-34, 36-39, 43,
    45, 47-51, 61, 64, 76, 84-85, 93, 106,
    114, 117-18, 120, 126, 133-34, 140,
    143, 152, 154-55, 159, 161-62, 166,
    171, 178, 180, 183, 185, 197, 199,
    205, 214, 221, 227, 229
Rochester Americans, 76
Rochester Chamber of Commerce, 183
Rochester Democrat and Chronicle, 86,
    151, 167
Rochester Music Hall of Fame, 227
Rochester Times-Union, 125
Rochester War Memorial, 104
Rock 'n' Roll Fantasy Camp, 207
Rock 'n' Roll Hall of Fame, 189-90

Rock of Ages, 203
Rodgers, Paul, 22, 40, 205
"Rock and Roll All Night," 41
Rolling Stone, 62, 89, 220, 229-30
Rolling Stones, 13-18, 24, 56, 79, 84, 86,
    130, 207
Romford, England, 16
Roth, David Lee, 123
Rough Diamonds No. 1, 225
Roxy Music, 96
Rumors, 92, 171
Rundgren, Todd, 21

S

Sacramento, 121
San Francisco, 28, 30
Santana, 199
Saturday Night Live, 66
"Say You Will," 119, 226
Schumacher, Joel, 129
Scotland, 106
Seaver, Tom, 5
Seger, Bob, 79
Sgt. Pepper, 22
Shadow King, 136-37, 143, 213
Showstoppers, 32
Silver Stadium, 118-19
Simple Minds, 170
Sinatra, Frank, 2, 209
Sinclair, John, 92
Singapore, 88
Smith, Kate, 78
Snider, Duke, 5
Songwriters Hall of Fame, 191-93, 227
Sonny James Orchestra, 1
"Soul Doctor," 145
South Africa, 106-7
Southern Tier region, 2
Sparacino, Andrew, 15
Spector, Phil, 20
Spencer Speedway, 185
Spevak, Jeff, 151, 167
Spooky Tooth, 33, 47-48, 53-54, 84, 190
Springsteen, Bruce, 60, 62, 107-8, 122,
    150, 191, 205, 208
Squier, Billy, 127
St. James Infirmary, 25, 27-28, 30

Stanley Cup, 77
Stanwyck, Barbara, 117
Starr, Ringo, 21, 190
Star-Spangled Banner, The, 191, 209
Stearns, Dave, 85
Stella Dallas Star, 117
Stern, Howard, 146
Steve Miller Band, 124, 127
Stevens, Cat, 36
Stewart, Rod, 34
"Stick Around," 37
Still Haven't Found What I'm Looking
    For," 124, 223
Storm Front, 149
Stranger, 166
"Street Thunder," 110
Strong Memorial Hospital, x
Sullivan, Ed, 16, 19
Summer Olympics, 109
Sunset Marquis, 143
Supremes, The, 204
Sutherland, Kiefer, 129
Sutton, Derek, 36
Switzerland, 88, 189
Syracuse, 22, 29, 36
Syracuse University, 6, 230

T

"Take Me To Your Leader," 50
Taking It to the Streets, 69
Taylor, James, 38
Taylor, Jim, 34-35, 37, 42, 71, 205
Taylor, Margaret, 113
Temptations, The, 204
Ten Years After, 39-40
Terrific, Tom, 5
Texas, 206
"That Was Yesterday," 114, 225
The Ed Sullivan Show, 19
The Tonight Show, 186
The Very Best of Foreigner… and Beyond,
    145, 224
The Voice, 50, 203
Thin Lizzy, 136
Thomas, Mickey, 201
Three Dog Night, 28
Tokyo, 174, 177

Tom Petty and the Heartbreakers, 206
Tony & The Knighthawks, 23
Top New Artist, 227
Torme, Mel, 8
Toronto Globe and Mail, 107
Toronto Star, 132
Toto, 92
Traffic, 19, 32, 34, 205
Travis, Randy, 21
Trigger, 53
"True Blue Love," 135, 224
Trump, Donald, 98
Tull, Jethro, 36, 38
Turgon, Bruce, 31, 39, 121, 123, 126,
    136, 149, 166, 171
Turner, Joe Lynn, 135
Tyler, Steven, 118

U

U2, 124, 223
Uncle Phil, 10
Union City, 176
United Kingdom, 104, 148, 191, 223-24
United States, 110, 128, 169, 174, 189,
    223-24
"Until the End of Time," 226
Unusual Heat, 143
Upton Horns, 126
"Urgent," 100, 102-4, 115, 118-19, 157,
    205, 220, 225

V

Valenti's Furniture Store, 44, 49, 120,
    181
Valentine, Kevin, 136
Van Halen, 123
Vancouver, 169
Vanilla Fudge, 105
Vartan, Sylvie, 53
Vaughan, Sarah, 21
VH1, 131, 166, 209, 230
Village Voice, 103
Voila, 77
Volkswagen, 22

W

"Wait Until Next Year," 6

"Waiting For A Girl Like You," 104-6, 110-111, 140, 145, 196, 209, 225
Walker, Junior, 102-3
Wallace, Ian, 84
Wallenda, Delilah, 84
War Memorial, xi, 15, 17, 76, 86, 104, 117
War Memorial Auditorium, 7
Washington, D.C., 70
Water Street Music Hall, 166
Welcome to the Revolution, 226
West Virginia, 39, 72
West Palm Beach, 145
Westchester County, 20, 52, 54, 65, 76, 91, 93-94, 116, 118
Westchester County Airport, 118
Whitesnake, 136
Wills, Rick, 96, 111
Wilson, Ann, 81
Wilson, Nancy, 81

Wings, 22, 119
Winwood, Steve, 205
"With Heaven on Our Side," 145, 226
WNEW-FM, 60
Wonderwheel, 54
Woodstock, 56, 79, 147
Wright, Betty, 80
Wright, Gary, 47, 54
Wurlitzer, 122

Y

Yankees, 5
Yarman & Erbe, 3
YouTube, 131

Z

Zander, Robin, 145
Zimmer, A.D., 197
ZZ Top, 190

About the Authors

LOU GRAMM rose from humble, working-class roots in Rochester, New York, to become one of rock 'n' roll's most distinctive and popular voices. As the powerhouse lead vocalist and co-songwriter for the iconic band Foreigner and for his own group, Gramm helped churn out seven multi-platinum albums and 21 Top 40 singles, including "Cold As Ice," "Feels Like the First Time," "Juke Box Hero," "I Want to Know What Love Is," "Urgent," "Midnight Blue," and "Double Vision." *Rolling Stone* magazine called him "the Pavarotti of the power rock ballad" and he was inducted into the Songwriters Hall of Fame in 2013. A resident of suburban Rochester where he resides with his wife, Robyn, Gramm recently retired his band, but continues to sing his classic songs at special concerts and hopes to release some remastered and new material in the near future. He is the father of five children—Nick, Matt, Joe, Natalie, and Luciana.

SCOTT PITONIAK is a nationally honored journalist and best-selling author of more than 25 books. The Associated Press named him one of America's top sports columnists, and he has been inducted into five halls of fame. A native of Rome, New York, and a magna cum laude graduate of Syracuse University, Pitoniak has written three previous titles for Triumph Books, including retrospectives on Yankee Stadium and the Buffalo Bills. This is his first venture into the music world, and he's learned that there are many similarities between the dynamics of rock bands and sports teams—each has star players and supporting casts. Pitoniak resides in suburban Rochester with his wife, Beth. He is the father of two grown children, Amy and Christopher, and has two granddaughters, Camryn and Peyton